Pictorial History of the
Fleet Air Arm

Pictorial History
of the
Fleet Air Arm

JOHN D. R. RAWLINGS

LONDON

IAN ALLAN LTD

First Published 1973
Second impression 1974

ISBN 0 7110 0436 6

Published by Ian Allan Ltd, Shepperton, Surrey
and printed in the United Kingdom by
A. Wheaton & Co. Exeter

Contents

Introduction

As these words are being written an act of incredible folly is taking place. At a time when the Soviet Navy is growing stronger at a rapid rate and is embarking on aircraft carrier construction herself, and when Britain's few remaining overseas air bases are becoming less and less tenable, the British Government is preparing HMS *Eagle*, one of Britain's only two Fleet Carriers, for the scrap yard and dispersing her squadron personnel with the consequent dilution of expertise built up over the years. This is typical of the inner battle against her friends that the Fleet Air Arm has always had to fight in addition to taking on the Queen's enemies as will be seen from a perusal of these pages. It is a stirring and fascinating story, that of the Fleet Air Arm, typifying the best traditions of the British services down the years and a story packed full of worthwhile lessons for everyone concerned with the welfare and security of our nation, provided they have eyes to see and ears to hear and whose hearts are not hardened to factual truth.

The photographs and text herein reflect the help given me by very many members of the Fleet Air Arm, all of whom it would be impossible to acknowledge. I would like to thank the various ships' companies who from time to time have given me facilities to sail, and fly, with them and the shore stations, too, whose willing and enthusiastic co-operation has gone to make this book possible. I am indebted to several books already published which have assisted my researches, not least Hugh Popham's *Into Wind* which provides such an excellent chart to the ways of the Fleet Air Arm, and David Brown's *Carrier Operations in World War Two*. On the photographic side I must mention the generosity of R. C. Jones who liberally opened his not inconsiderable library of photographs at my disposal and from whom so many of those used have come. I have endeavoured to give acknowledgement to the sources of the photographs but where these have been taken from old photograph albums it is not always possible to trace the original copyright; if I have failed with any of these I ask for understanding forgiveness. Many FAA and ex-FAA members have lent me photograph albums and these are duly acknowledged against the appropriate photographs. My thanks go out to all who have helped.

J. D. R. Rawlings

Just Four
Men

'A grain of mustard seed . . . which indeed is the least of all the seeds; but when it is grown . . . becometh a tree, so that the birds of the air come and lodge in the branches thereof.' (St Matthew Ch 13)

Although the proper beginnings of British Naval Aviation rest with four Naval Officers a brief preamble is necessary, in order to keep the record straight and give credit where credit is due, into the happenings arising out of an Admiralty appointment of 1908.

It was in that year that Captain R. H. S. Bacon, DSO (as he then was) proposed that a new post, that of Naval Air Assistant, be created within the Admiralty Staff. The First Sea Lord's approval was obtained in the New Year and an Inspecting Captain of Aircraft was appointed, Captain Murray Sueter, and given an Assistant, Commander Oliver Schwann. The aircraft they had been appointed to inspect was, in fact, to be an airship for which a contract was given to Vickers Sons and Maxim of Barrow-in-Furness in May, 1909. This was a most ambitious project for the plans envisaged a rigid dirigible of 700,000 cubic feet capacity and a length exceeding 500ft. In the two years that this craft was a-building the popular talk of the times had dubbed the Senior Service's aeronautical venture the *Mayfly*, a temptation which fate could not resist. September 29th, 1911 was scheduled as the 'roll-out' date for the Mayfly and it dawned as a typical autumn day with a typical autumn gale. Nothing daunted, the doors were opened and Mayfly eased into the open for its trial flight. Disaster overtook it however before it had even left its hangar for the wind caught the nose and swung the airship round so that the hangar doorpost acted as a lever and broke the ship's back. The craft was destroyed, the Admiralty proposed no further money for this venture and the *Mayfly* began and ended its life in those few moments.

The Admiralty, which was by no means wholeheartedly in favour of aviation anyway, became somewhat disenchanted with lighter-than-air flying after this set-back and two years elapsed before airships again appeared in their programmes. However, those with eyes to see and minds to understand were taking note of a much less ambitious experiment which had, in a sense, been forced upon the Admiralty by the public-spiritedness of one of the early British aviators. Mr Francis McClean had for some time been running his own flying establishment at Eastchurch on the Isle of Sheppey and early in 1911 he offered two of his aircraft (Short biplanes) to the Admiralty for instructing naval aviators and G. B. Cockburn offered his services free as an instructor. This seemed a cheap way of feeling its way into heavier-than-air flying and so the Admiralty took advantage of the offer to train four officers as pilots—four, selected from some 500 applicants. On these four fell the mantle of proving to a sceptical Navy that aviation, the rich man's toy, might be of some small service to Great Britain's Senior Service; their names were Lts R. Gregory, A. M. Longmore and C. R. Samson, RN and Lt E. L. Gerrard, Royal Marines Light Infantry.

These four assembled at Eastchurch on March 1st, 1911 to begin their flying instruction. This could only be carried on at dawn and sunset when the wind was light and the Shorts could stagger on and off the sloping field at Eastchurch. Instruction was given by the instructor flying the aircraft and the pupil, strapped to a ladder-like contraption behind him, reaching over and putting his finger on the stick to 'get the feel'. Despite this, or perhaps because of it, first solos took place after two or three hours flying and although flying was restricted to times when the wind was 10mph or below, two of the four naval pilots (Samson and Longmore) gained their Royal Aero Club Certificates, the then equivalent of PPL and 'Wings' rolled into one, on April 24th, less than two months from their arrival at Eastchurch and their colleagues shortly afterwards. They were now able to fly passengers so, unofficially, began spreading the enthusiasm for flying amongst their brother officers stationed at nearby Sheerness Dockyard. However whilst naval aviation was confined to flights around the Isle of Sheppey no one above the rank of Lieutenant was likely to be impressed with the aeroplane as a naval weapon so in June the first cross-country was flown—fifty odd miles to Brooklands, a journey which involved a forced landing both ways and was shared between Samson and Longmore, the enterprise taking three days. All this activity was likely to fold up, however, when the six months' detachment to Eastchurch for the four officers ended but with such forceful characters as Samson, activities did not end and the Admiralty were persuaded to rent ten acres of Eastchurch and to purchase the two Short biplanes from Mr McClean together with another Short, nicknamed 'The Dud'. Twelve naval ratings were assigned to Eastchurch to learn the rudiments of maintenance and four more officers sent to learn how to fly from the first four; the first stage in forming Naval Aviation was ended.

By comparison with other nations the Admiralty had given little enough to aviation but what they had given was exploited to the full by the resourcefulness of the first four aviators. By keeping the training machine turning they now devoted themselves to the far more difficult task of applying this new art of flying to the problems of naval warfare—a herculean task indeed.

Eastchurch was also used by the makers of their aircraft, the Short Bros and one of the three brothers, Horace, had spent considerable time during the first course instructing the officers in the theories of flight and of engines and generally keeping them abreast of all that was going on. Naval flying, by its very nature, would sooner or later involve aircraft coming into contact with the sea; to prepare for this eventuality Longmore began working with Oswald Short on experiments to enable water landings to take place. In November, 1911 Lt Longmore flew one of the Shorts, fitted with airbags around the undercarriage, and alighted on the Medway successfully, to the mild surprise of all. Brought ashore on Grain Island the pilot wiped the engine dry of spray and took off to return to Eastchurch. Similarly airbags were being used in experiments carried out at Barrow at the same time. Cdr Oliver Schwann was attached to Vickers' dockyard and had been Assistant in supervising the rise and fall of the *Mayfly*; he had since designed airbags to be fitted to an Avro biplane and these were built at local expense. His flights into the dock at Barrow (literally) were not conspicuously successful as much, it has been said, due to his rudimentary knowledge of flying as to the efficacy of the device. More spectacularly successful was Samson's next contribution to naval flying; on January 10th, 1912 he flew a Short biplane across the Medway and alighted on the beach, the aircraft was lightered out to the cruiser HMS *Africa* on the bows of which had been erected inclined staging over the gun-turret. The Short was hoisted on to this and in due course Samson, with his engine running, let the machine run down the staging and climbed away successfully to Eastchurch—Britain's first deck take-off had been successfully accomplished. Their Lordships at the Admiralty were not stirred unduly; this take-off had meant that the *Africa*'s fore turret was unusable and such an idea was unthinkable to the policy-makers of that day and, in fact, the argument dogged naval aviation development for several decades later. The surface of Admiralty policy may not have been rippled as yet but the doggedness of the few enthusiasts in the Navy was by no means discouraged and events of 1912 gave them sufficient scope (and hope) for pressing on.

For at the same time that Samson was sliding off HMS *Africa* and Longmore and Schwann were making more intimate contact with the sea and a Lt H. A. Williamson was delivering a paper enumerating the advantages of aircraft for submarine-spotting and outlining the principle of the aircraft-carrier, the Mother of Parliaments was rudely awakened to the fact that whilst Germany was in aviation business in a big way with Zeppelins and

France had over 200 military aviators, the combined flying personnel of the Army and Navy totalled nineteen. What would now be termed a crash programme was initiated through a Technical Sub-Committee despite which action was taken within four months, action which in a sense created something potentially greater than was realised at the time, a third service. This was the Royal Flying Corps, formed by Royal Warrant on April 13th, 1912, to contain a Naval Wing and a Military Wing intended to act as one force rather than two different branches of different services and one can speculate as to developments had this remained so. Unfortunately, neither the Generals nor the Admirals were sufficiently sold on aviation yet to see it as the potent force it might become and, realising the limited potential it contained if restricted to the advances immediately in sight, both Services determined to retain their own aviation interests whilst paying lip-service to the new Corps. In point of fact this lip-service took the form of participation in the Central Flying School, formed at Upavon on May 13th, 1912 with Capt Godfrey Paine, RN, as Commandant and two of the first four Naval aviators, Longmore and Gerrard, as instructors. Inevitably, being on Salisbury Plain, the CFS became Army-orientated and it soon became apparent that the Senior Service had little intention of leaving its aviation future in the hands of a third force, despite their reluctance to see any real future in aviation. Consequently, flying training continued at Eastchurch in addition to Upavon and work went on apace to fit the aeroplane to the uses of the Fleet. Second of the shipborne take-offs was arranged, not this time as part of a development programme but within the public glare of a royal visit to the naval exercises. So when HM King George V appeared in the Royal Yacht *Victoria and Albert*, Samson, now a Commander, was using two Shorts with floats, one an old pusher, the other a tractor biplane and these were confidently flown on and off the water in Weymouth Bay. Then the old pusher seaplane was hoisted on to the bows of the battleship *Hibernia* and, with the ship sailing at fifteen knots, Samson successfully flew off and subsequently landed on the water. After the Review the Naval contingent returned to Eastchurch aboard the *Hibernia*. Whilst passing Dover Cdr Samson again flew off, intending to fly back to Eastchurch but he was forced down on to the water off Westgate. His Short was taken in tow by a destroyer and successfully returned to Sheerness harbour, sufficient testimony to the toughness and practicability of the floats which had replaced the air-bag experiments of the previous years. The following month a Short Tractor was flown off HMS *London* in the Channel by Lt L'E. Malone and two other Shorts were flown on a 196 mile cross-country from Eastchurch round the coast to Portsmouth. This was capped a few miles later by a 250 mile flight from Portsmouth to Harwich with a stop at Dover for the night.

This was the measure of progress since the first cross-country from

Eastchurch to Brooklands a year before; sufficient to encourage the proponents of aviation within the Navy to press on with the considerable problems facing them. The remainder of 1912 saw attempts at some of these; in June and September, 1912 experiments at Rosyth and Harwich were made into the possibilities of spotting submarines from the air, the inimitable Cdr Samson had taken a 100lb bomb aloft and dropped it without ill effects to his somewhat frail craft and the W/T explosion that was surging through the world had invaded the Naval Wing with the possibilities of air-to-ship W/T being tentatively explored.

Failing a suitable device to use in the air the first W/T experiments were carried out at a shore station on Burntwick Island where conditions were made as realistically like those in an aircraft as possible. A Short seaplane had been fitted with transmitter and receiver for the May exercises at Weymouth during which ranges of three to five miles were obtained, sufficient promise to warrant further experiment. Cdr Samson used the same aircraft for further experiments in the Harwich area but at this time the overriding problem was the weight of the equipment in the aircraft of the day, affected as they were by every ounce of surplus equipment. What had been accomplished so far encouraged the Admiralty sufficiently to appoint one officer, Lt L. R. Fitzmaurice, to full-time development work on airborne W/T; his first task, however, turned out to be a detachment to Farnborough to supervise the W/T equipment in the Army's airship *Gamma* for military manoeuvres.

Despite their early experience with lighter-than-air craft the Admiralty had to concede that such aircraft were performing well in the hands of others, notably the Germans, and on paper had much to recommend them for overwater and long-range flying; aviation, do not forget, was still so much in its infancy that no one could at this stage tell which was the dead end of development, heavier-than-air or lighter-than-air, although each had its fanatics. On September 25th, 1912 the Admiralty played safe by resurrecting the Naval Airship Section and putting Cdr E. A. D. Masterman in command with three Lieutenants and some ratings in his care. To catch up with events they were at first attached to the Military Wing's airship section at Farnborough; experience gained there saw plans blossoming for 1913 with an airship station to be established at Kingsnorth (in the Medway area, the cradle of British naval flying) and an 'Astra Torres' non-rigid ordered from the Astra company in Paris, due to arrive in the Spring. Before 1912 ended, however, they had received their first machine by the purchase of Naval Airship No 2 from Mr T. E. Willows, a small non-rigid which had been the Willows No 4.

To crown all this activity, in November, 1912 the Air Department was formed within the Admiralty, ostensibly to administer the Naval Wing of the RFC, but which in practice went ahead with policy-making for the

Navy's own Air Service of the future—operations were seen to fall into two classes, fleet and patrol work and a draft list of naval aircraft duties drawn up, a visionary list indeed at this stage but one which was to see fruition, if not in World War I, in the second great holocaust which lay ahead of the Service. These duties were:

1. Distant recce with the Fleet at sea
2. Recce of enemy coasts (flying off cruisers or 'aeroplane ships')
3. Assisting destroyers to detect and destroy submarines
4. Detecting mine-layers at work and mines already laid
5. Locating hostile ships in friendly sea lanes
6. Assisting submarines in searching for vessels to attack
7. Attacking enemy aircraft observing the Fleet
8. Defending dockyards and naval installations from air attack

In fact at the close of the year proposals were submitted for the building of an aircraft-carrier to designs prepared by Wm Beardmore & Co Ltd of Dalmuir in consultation with Capt Sueter; due to its far-reaching implications these designs were deferred to a conference on the subject, a conference which was in fact never held.

Such notions were far from reality, it is true, at the close of 1912 but remembering that the major part of the Navy had no use for aviation, the strides made by the naval aviators in the first two years of activity were formidable.

Sir Arthur Longmore, one of the first four naval aviators, writing in his memoirs *From Sea to Sky* stated 'I have always regarded 1913 as the year when the Navy began to be interested (in aviation)'. The results of all the labours of the dedicated band of enthusiasts had brought naval aviation to a point where the Admiralty could see a possible operational use for it. Henceforward, although there were many battles still to be fought, aviation had a small but energetic lobby in Whitehall. Obviously the North Sea was to be the focal point of future naval action in the view of those who could see war upon the horizon and so if Naval Aviation was to play any operational part it must be focused around this area. Whilst conceding that the ideal would be for aircraft to operate from ships it was felt that, at this stage of the game, aircraft and ship development was such that this was only practicable in calm conditions and by reducing the flexibility of action of the Fleet; so the Admiralty's first move in 1913 was to establish air stations around the coast from which naval aircraft could fly out over the North Sea for action. Captain Murray Sueter was given the task of establishing these and he set about looking for suitable sites. What was required was a location with a beach or sea frontage of 450/500ft suitable for launching and recovering seaplanes, land adjacent which would make a suitable aerodrome and, most important of all, buildings already erected which would make suitable accommodation for the personnel for so slender was Captain Sueter's budget that it would run to precious few quarters. It was no coincidence then, that he looked closely at Coastguard stations as these had similar requirements apart from the land aerodromes. To soften the blow to the Coastguard service it was pointed out that naval flying could take over some of the coastguard duties; accordingly three out of the first four coastal air stations arose out of the availability of cottages as accommodation.

First of these Air Stations to open was not far from Eastchurch, in fact at the Isle of Grain. Lt Gregory was put in command of one at Great Yarmouth which would also administer the one to be established at Felixstowe. These three stations were to cover the southern North Sea and the Channel area around the Kent Coast; the fourth, at Calshot covered further along the Channel. In theory the Naval Wing of the RFC was now ready for active service; in practice the Admiralty was making sure of establishing its own Air Branch of the Navy in independence of the Royal Flying Corps. This was made even clearer on May 7th, 1913 when the Naval Air Service, as it now called itself, commissioned its first parent ship an adapted cruiser HMS *Hermes* with Torpedo Boat No 23 allocated to serve with her. Captain G. W. Vivian was placed in command aboard and his empire included all naval flying, ashore and afloat.

It is significant that this accelerated development of the 'Naval Wing' into what was in effect a new, if small, branch of the Navy took place whilst the First Lord's chair in the Admiralty was occupied by one Winston Churchill, an enthusiast himself who had early on insisted on flying with the early naval aviators and encouraged them more perhaps than the professional sailors. It was at this time, too, that the Navy's thoughts turned to expanding their lighter-than-air commitment, despite opposition by those who remembered the *Mayfly*. Funding was made for two rigids and six non-rigids—the two rigids were to be Zeppelins, one built by Vickers (eventually to become R9) and one in Germany, the six non-rigids were to be one German Parseval, one Italian Forlanini, two from Armstrong-Whitworth's and two from Vickers. With this fleet the Kingsnorth Station would have become a hive of activity but of course, due to the War in 1914, only the three Vickers airships materialised.

Lieutenant Fitzmaurice, the W/T man, visited the Eiffel Tower W/T station in 1913 and there he found what he had been looking for, a light-weight (70lb) alternator and using this he was able to provide an experimental installation which, flying over Dover, gave a range of twenty miles with some random reception at up to 45 miles. Further installations were made and one, in Short Seaplane No 20, went to Great Yarmouth Air Station for operational use. This particular aircraft used its wireless to good

13

effect in May whilst escorting the Royal Yacht from Flushing to Port Victoria in the Thames, being in touch with Naval Air Station Isle of Grain all the way.

All this provided sound evidence of progress. How far the Naval Air Service was operational or not was put to the test in the Naval Manoeuvres of 1913, the first in which the existence of aircraft were admitted although limitations, which would now seem severe, were put on the part they could play in the War Game (a Game which, incidentally, the German Command recognised as a preparation for dealing with the German Fleet). In this battle, then, aircraft were considered immune from attack, either from ships or other aircraft but to counterbalance this they were only to be used for reconnaissance and not to be considered as capable of dropping on or firing at the Fleet; which, considering the types of aircraft involved, was probably an accurate estimate. The two forces and their dispositions of air power were 'Red' Force with HMS *Hermes*, complete with Cdr Samson and two seaplanes and Great Yarmouth with three seaplanes and one landplane and 'Blue' Force with Air Stations at Leven and Cromarty. The latter was an interesting example of advanced thinking in that it took the form of a mobile Air Station. At the beginning of May it existed only on paper and Lt Longmore was sent north to establish it. He found a suitable site at the Coastguard Station whence portable Bessoneau hangars were lightered from Sheerness and erected. In July the complement of three seaplanes arrived, a Farman Shorthorn, a Borel monoplane (with rowlocks beside the cockpits so that the crew could row themselves home!), and a Sopwith Tractor.

Knowing that this was a crucial test for aviation in the eyes of the Navy the aviators made use of every opportunity to show their prowess. Cdr Samson on *Hermes*, with his customary gusto, flew two successful sorties on the first day in Short No 81 and repeated his efforts on the second until fog clamped down. The Borel made one attempt to fly but could not get off the water and was wrecked the following day. Great Yarmouth's most successful efforts were by their one landplane, a Farman, which flew recces and sighted two submarines off Cromer—the floatplane flying was hampered by beaching difficulties. Leven and Cromarty flew regular coastal patrols the while. On the fourth day Great Yarmouth really came into its own spotting two submarines in the morning and a battleship and four destroyers off Smiths Knoll in the afternoon though the next day their Short Floatplane No 20 force-landed and was captured by Blue Force. On that day Cromarty made its first submarine sighting and Yarmouth clocked up its fifth. Thus ended the first phase. When the second phase opened the Air Service was able to do little as most aircraft were now in need of repair; only the irrepressible Cdr Samson got airborne from *Hermes* in No 81 but had engine failure and went down. As he had been using W/T most successfully the naval vessels were able to plot his position only to find that he and his observer had been picked up by the German collier *Clara Mennig*.

So ended the first practical test of Naval Aviation in action. Lessons had been learnt, amongst them being the difficulties of launching and retrieving seaplanes from ships in the open sea, the relatively short range cover which the coastal air stations could at present give and the high rate of attrition of the aircraft. Against these rather negative lessons had come out the effectiveness of W/T both for transmitting messages and for position finding in case of distress, the ease with which submarines could be sighted (a finding which led to increased development of this role) and the facility with which an Air Station could be set up at relatively short notice. During this Exercise the aviation side came more closely before the notice of the sea-going Navy and several Admirals, Jellicoe included, became airborne over their ships to their delight.

In the Autumn Cromarty Air Station was moved, lock stock and barrel down to Fort George at the more sheltered entrance to Inverness Firth. Calshot had not entered into the battle because it was out of the North Sea area and it was in fact the Station at which most of the experimental flying of new developments took place. The variety of experiment was enhanced by Admiralty policy which had been running counter to that laid down for the Royal Flying Corps which stated that military aeroplanes would be developed and built by the Royal Aircraft Factory, Farnborough and that the Military and Naval Wings were to order and use these machines. This had never appealed to the Admiralty and though they took a proportion of Farnborough types they felt free to buy from anywhere the aircraft they thought most suitable for their task. Thus French or British, biplane or monoplane, the naval fliers had the most effective aircraft available and certainly were better equipped with more advanced aircraft than the RFC, a situation which was repeated again in the early sixties. This independence and, in particular, the fostering of the British firms of Short Bros and Sopwiths was to have a pivotal effect on British aircraft procurement and development in the War which, at this time, was still looming on the horizon.

Early in January, 1914 the Grain Air Station was given an emergency call when the submarine A7 was in trouble off Plymouth. Cdr Seddon set off at once in a Maurice Farman and after a flight of five hours twenty minutes with one stop reached the spot. By then the emergency was over as the submarine had been found but this showed the possibilities of aircraft in this role. Had the Cattewater Air Station, Plymouth, then been in existence an aircraft could have been over the spot within minutes.

Naval aviators, though a part of the Silent Service, have never been at a loss where showmanship was concerned; maybe this was a tradition established by Cdr Samson whose feats have already been recorded in these pages. In April, 1914 he seized the opportunity of the Royal Visit to Paris to put up an impressive airborne escort for the Royal Yacht, eight aircraft of assorted types led by the Commander in a BE2; amongst the formation was Eng Lt Briggs in a Bleriot monoplane in which he had just previously raised the British altitude record to 14,920ft (no oxygen, an open cockpit and considerable frostbite).

Whilst the Air Stations were learning the bare necessities of life required to improve their effectiveness, developments went ahead at Calshot. A Sopwith pusher seaplane was fitted with a 1½pdr gun in the nose nacelle and successful firings were made by the gunnery officer, Lt Clarke Hall—despite this the installation was not proceeded with. Night flying was going ahead, too, most successes being obtained with a Sopwith BAT boat, more akin to a small flying boat than a seaplane, having a boat hull similar to the American Curtiss boat. Calshot became the focal point for all naval fliers in July with the arrival of the Royal Naval Review at Spithead. The month before what had become obvious for many months had been made an accomplished fact; the Admiralty had finally cleaved the Royal Flying Corps in two by establishing the Royal Naval Air Service which consisted of the Air Department (Admiralty), the Central Air Office, the Royal Naval Flying School and the Royal Naval Air Stations. The first Director of the Air Department was Capt Murray Sueter, CB who had been in naval aviation from the first tentative steps with the *Mayfly*. At last the Navy had forced itself free from all entangling red tape.

This Royal Review was of interest in that the Navy's seaplanes were moored in line together with the ships for the Review, probably the only time this was done, and then slipped their moorings and flew round the Fleet as part of the Review proceedings. Shortly after this, in response to pressure from the new Air Department, the first launching of a torpedo from an aircraft took place, Longmore, one of the first four, being the pilot. although it was successful this was merely a gesture and it would be a long time before such a flight could be made 'for real'. The next month Great Britain was at war; the grain of mustard seed which had been planted in 1911 with the training of just four officers to fly aeroplanes had grown indeed and whilst not yet strong or sturdy enough for the fowls of the air to come and lodge (there was no aircraft carrier as such yet) it had become a sturdy plant, blessed with more than its share of courage, ingenuity and forcefulness, qualities which were to the fore in the months ahead.

Put to the Test

'All these, mighty men of valour, . . . were apt to the war and to battle.'
(I Chronicles Ch 7)

With the outbreak of War in August, 1914 for all of three weeks the Naval Aviators indulged in no particularly warlike activity for the RNAS was marshalling itself for the months ahead. Longmore, from Calshot, went scouring the civilian training airfields at Brooklands, Hendon, Eastbourne and Shoreham, where he requisitioned fourteen miscellaneous aircraft. The Kingsnorth Air Station probably made the most significant contribution at this stage by putting up its two airships *Astra Torres* and *Parseval* on escort duties, flying with the convoys across the English Channel which were taking the British Army to France; these flew 12-hour patrols enabling an efficient eye to be kept for lurking German surface vessels and, under the right conditions, for U-boats as well.

But more than this was envisaged for the Royal Naval Air Service and on August 27th, 1914 Cdr Samson took his Eastchurch Wing, all ten aircraft, and landed on Ostend racecourse, moving to a more suitable field the next day. This became No 1 Wing RNAS and with the land battle in a fluid and highly unsatisfactory state there was little that the aircraft could do. The enterprising Samson, however, was certainly 'apt to the War' and acquired 350 infantry and artillery, an ammunition column and his beloved armoured cars. These vehicles, covered in boiler plate, were launched into battle with such verve as to hearten the natives of the area and harass the attacking Huns most effectively—a typically Samsonian activity but one which had little to further aeronautical participation. At home the coastal air stations had been called to readiness and were already patrolling their respective areas as far as weather and the serviceability of their matchbox-like aircraft permitted.

Once the land battle had been contained the RNAS was soon to be reinforced by Longmore bringing across every available aircraft at Hendon and Eastchurch to form the Dunkirk Wing, combined with Samson's ten aircraft which had retreated there from Ostend. The RNAS could now

F.A.A.—B

define its duties more clearly and these were established as opposition, both on the ground and in the air, to the Zeppelin force, in particular to impede their establishing a base in Belgium, to patrol the coast, particularly the ports of Ostend and Zeebrugge, and to prevent submarines being assembled at Brussels. To Samson's mind this meant attack and the Zeppelin sheds at two of the German bases just within reach of the Wing were tempting targets indeed; although the first two attempts were ill-starred the third raid in early October by Cdr Spenser-Grey and Lt Marix in two Sopwith Tabloids, tiny 25ft span single-seat biplanes which could carry a small load of 20lb bombs, setting out from the airfield at Antwerp whilst under enemy shellfire was very different. Spenser Grey lost his way and bombed Cologne railway station instead but Marix, finding the Zeppelin station, dived to 600ft and dropped his two 20lb bombs on one of the sheds. To his delight an immense explosion brought flames up to 500ft for inside had been Zeppelin Z.IX—scarcely can there have been a more economical bombing raid but its effect was to prove to those with eyes to see the effectiveness of strategic bombing. This success spawned a brain-child which appeared in November. Four Avro 504's, together with crews, entrained and went south to Belfort, in the Vosges. Here the aircraft were prepared in conditions of great secrecy and after a week's wait conditions enabled the four aircraft to take off, bombed up with four twenty-pounders each, although the fourth broke his tailskid and had to abort the sortie. The other three, piloted by Babington, Briggs and Sippe, carried on to their target, the Zeppelin Centre at Friedrichshafen on Lake Constance. In they went to bomb the target, Briggs being brought down in the attack, and when they left, one shed with a new Zeppelin inside had received a direct hit and the gas-plant was totally destroyed. These two, Babington and Sippe, returned safely. As a result, the Germans maintained heavy defences on Friedrichshafen from then on although it was never again attacked.

This was the most spectacular of the RNAS's attacks but it was not the only one carried out by the Dunkirk Wing. This Wing conceived its task of defence against U-boat and Zeppelin activities entirely in terms of attack, laying the foundation for the policy of strategic bombing which paid such dividends at later dates. Slowly this Wing of ill-assorted aircraft built up the tempo of its raids on the Zeebrugge and Ostend areas to hamper the growing menace of U-boats in the Channel and North Sea. Thus was the Royal Naval Air Service to begin its career, by mapping out the way ahead for air forces of the future to learn the effectiveness of strategic bombing, a lesson that was not lost on one of the early Army aviators, a man by the name of Trenchard. One further strategic raid of 1914 deserves mention here because it goes into history as the first ship-mounted strategic bombing raid. Captain Murray Sueter, the father of naval aviation, saw in this an opportunity to vindicate to the sceptics in the Admiralty the value of his naval air service. Although planned for November it was not until Christmas Day that it took place (bad weather had held it up); a considerable task force had been built up comprising cruisers, destroyers, and a screen of submarines but the centre of it all was the three ex-Channel steamers which had been converted as seaplane carriers, *Engadine, Riviera* and *Empress*. Each of these carried three seaplanes which, early on Christmas morn were hoisted on to the calm North Sea waters. Of the nine, seven eventually became airborne, three Short Type 74's, two Short Folders and two Short Type 135's. Their target was the Airship sheds at Cuxhaven but this they were unable to find so they found targets of opportunity, one the centre of Wilhelmshaven, others cruisers, submarines and seaplane sheds. Damage was slight although one useful by-product was the collision of two German warships caused by the dismay at finding British aircraft overhead. Judged by tangible results the raid was a failure but as the precursor of future operations its value was immense and was not lost on the ones and twos in the Navy whose vision stretched into the decades ahead.

In any Service there are not only the pioneering units, pushing ahead the development of tactics and methods but the humdrum units daily carrying out their allotted tasks. Amongst these were the Coastal Air Stations, of which Great Yarmouth had been the precursor under Gregory. These were maintaining, as far as practicable against weather and local conditions which were hard and primitive in many ways, regular patrols both of the coastline and as far out to sea as the fuel tanks of their heterogeneous fleet of aircraft would allow. The Station at Calshot, started by Longmore, had now become largely a training station, its experimental and development role being taken over by Felixstowe. Now that the RNAS was established on a war footing some re-organisation of its organisation was undertaken. Wisely, the coastal air stations were left in their rather flexible status. Samson's Dunkirk Wing became No 3 Squadron, RNAS a No 1 Squadron formed at Gosport under Longmore and a No 2 at Eastchurch under Gerrard—it is interesting to note that these first four naval aviators had kept themselves in the business end of the RNAS rather than becoming desk-ridden at the Admiralty. Before the end of the year further Air Stations had appeared at Killingholme, Skegness, Scapa and Thurso; as a general rule patrols were flown at 'Dawn', 'Midday' and 'Sunset' and other times only if alarms and excursions occurred. Aircraft began to be armed, some with 'a rifle poked through a hole in the fabric by the passenger', others, as already recounted, with 16 and 20lb bombs. Many flights ended in forced-landings and it is not surprising that no sightings were made in 1914. At times the Air Stations would have all their aircraft unserviceable and this was the case when Great Yarmouth was shelled by a German battle-cruiser on November 7th, 1914, an embarrassing situation for the fledgling Air Station.

It is now necessary to turn attention once more to the lighter-than-air side of Naval affairs. The early successes of the German U-boats and the apparent inability of the Navy to cope had brought a conference into being of airship specialists as soon as Admiral Fisher became First Sea Lord in October, 1914 with the result that early in 1915 his first brain-child, Submarine Scout Airship No 1 appeared in March, 1915 and only eighteen days work had been taken to complete it. Like many a brilliant weapon the concept was amazingly simple—a gas bag, of 60,000 cu ft capacity was constructed and beneath it slung a BE2 fuselage complete with engine (although the prototype had the envelope from the Willows No 4 in order to speed trials). No fault of an incurable nature was found and so production of fifty was soon ordered and although the prototype crashed whilst low-flying the principle had been proved. 1915 saw the introduction of these into service and their main value was to keep the U-boats' heads down. Few were destroyed by them but in keeping the U-boats below the surface they provided a valuable limitation on their operation, as far as the SS ships could provide for only nine were in service by the time 1915 ended.

1915 saw the menacing success of another of the Navy's enemies, the Zeppelin. The first raid on the UK came on January 19th and the RNAS, to whom had been entrusted the aerial defence of the country, were powerless. The second raid came on April 15th and although the East Anglian air stations put aircraft up the Zeppelins continued to roam at will across the area—the third raid served to underline the impotence of the Service. It was known that the Zeppelins liked to make a landfall by dusk so as to know their position so trawlers at Yarmouth were fitted with Sopwith Schneider seaplanes and these went fifty miles out into the North Sea from whence, in calm weather, the aircraft were to roam in search of approaching airships. No sightings were ever made on these operations, the net result being the torpedoing of one trawler. The impunity of the German airship fleets was made plain when, on May 10th, LZ 38 sat in the Thames Estuary and dropped 124 bombs on Southend. Eleven aircraft attempted to intercept it but failed to make contact. It became increasingly clear that greater flexibility of landplanes was needed so Emergency Landing Grounds were set up in East Anglia and most attempts at defence were henceforth made with landplanes. This policy brought a success on June 7th, 1915 with the destruction of LZ 37; Flt Sub Lt R. A. J. Warneford sighted it over Ostend whilst off on a bombing raid in his Morane Parasol 3253 so he climbed above it and dropped his bombs there. The subsequent explosion destroyed LZ 37 and all but destroyed Warneford who was blown out of control, however he forced-landed behind the German lines, mended the broken fuel pipe before being captured and flew back to Dunkirk. For this he received the RNAS's first VC. This was as a member of No 1 Wing which Longmore had taken across to Dunkirk at first to supplement and then to replace Samson's Wing, known variously as No 3 (Aeroplane) Sqn or No 3 Wing.

This latter was withdrawn from the Western Front and proceeded across France to Marseilles and then by sea to that most desperate of actions—Gallipoli. Arriving on March 24th, 1915 it was only a few days' later that they were flying recce sorties from the small, bare airfield at Tenedos. One of their first tasks was to spot for the guns of HMS *London* and, despite little or no W/T equipment, improvised (an art in which the RNAS was perforce a master) sufficiently to make the task possible. Terms of reference were reconnaisance with the land and sea forces but once again Samson had his own ideas and began bombing the Turkish positions, ordering his men always to fly armed when on recce and to find targets of opportunity, not that the size of the bombs had much impact over and above a morale weapon. More important was the photographic contribution made by the Wing which gave the commanders what they failed to possess, accurate maps of the area where they were fighting. But it was not only Samson's Wing that was in action in the Dardanelles. In a sense the more important aspect of the affair from the Naval Air point of view was that HMS *Ark Royal* was on the scene. This vessel, a converted merchantman, was the next stage onwards in the development of the aircraft-carrier in that it had a flying-off deck (which, of course, was never used). This vessel had preceded 3 Wing to Gallipoli and, hoisting her seaplanes overboard, attempted to provide a recce force for the Naval units, an unsuccessful task in that weather conditions more often than not precluded launchings—one valuable contribution that the Short and Wight seaplanes from *Ark Royal* did make was to go mine-spotting and this was of value to the Fleet. Following this the vessel went a-roaming around the Aegean looking for Turks and subsequently farther afield in the Middle East, having been relieved on the Gallipoli station by *Ben-my-Chree*, the second 'carrier' with a flying-off deck. When, eventually, amphibious landings were made at Cape Helles the 3 Wing crews threw themselves into frantic activity spotting and supporting as they could but there was little they could do to prevent the massacre of their countrymen below—interdiction as such was just not on the cards at that time. Samson's men were fast wearing themselves and their machines out when a U-boat, *U-21*, appeared on the scene. After two torpedoings the fleet sheltered in Mudros harbour and Samson was called upon for help. In spite of sightings and an attack his Wing was unable to despatch *U-21*.

Ben-my-Chree, being a faster vessel than *Ark Royal*, was not imprisoned in Mudros and went about her ways; whilst doing this, almost casually, she notched up some more 'firsts' in the development of naval aviation. On June 12th, 1915 Flt Cdr C. H. K. Edmonds flew one of the ship's Short 184s with a torpedo slung between the floats and made a classic attack on a large Turkish vessel, the torpedo found its mark amidships. Two months later this performance was repeated by Edmonds and Flt Lt G. B. Dacre found a ship and a tug, Edmonds sank the ship and Dacre, forced down on the water by the weight of the torpedo, taxied in the direction of the tug, loosed the torpedo and was thus able to take off once more; his aim was good and as he went up the tug went down. Had these momentous efforts happened in the North Sea or the English Channel torpedo-dropping would have proceeded apace but because it was in an area which was already heartily disliked at the Admiralty the news was ignored and no further torpedo attacks were made for the rest of the War. As already mentioned, the RNAS element was all but played out in the theatre yet it was here, before 1915 was out, that the RNAS's second VC was won. By now the fighting had been complicated by Bulgaria joining Germany and thus providing a direct link with the Turks. The RNAS was told to destroy a bridge which might hamper the supply lines from Germany and many unsuccessful attempts were made. During one attack an aircraft was forced down and the pilot was about to be captured by Bulgarians. The pilot of the other, Bell-Davies, landed beside him and picked him from under the Bulgarian's noses.

The problems which beset the Wing in the Dardanelles were largely caused by an almost total lack of supply of replacement equipment for the unit. Though worse there, the same problem to a lesser scale bedevilled the whole of the RNAS during 1915. Fifty SS airships had been ordered, only nine arrived, fifty Naval Air Stations had been commissioned by August, 1915 but each one was struggling with an ill-assorted agglomeration of aircraft. Of seagoing ships capable of operating aircraft there were none other than those already named.

At this juncture a new name comes on the scene of Naval Aviation. He had been a Lieutenant in the Navy before the War and was invalided out and this man, Lt John C. Porte, was working in America with Glenn Curtiss on flying-boats when War was declared. He immediately returned and joined up once more, being a pilot he naturally gravitated to the RNAS. With him he brought a firm conviction in the efficacy of the flying-boat, a variant of the aeroplane which had received scant attention from the Admiralty up to this time. By dint of persuasiveness he obtained their permission to purchase two H4 flying-boats from Curtiss and use them from Felixstowe Air Station over the North Sea. At first these two aircraft proved little better than the seaplanes but Porte had ideas of his own and set about modifying and arming them until, with improved alterations to the hull and Rolls-Royce engines in place of the Curtiss OX-5's, something promising ensued. Altogether the RNAS purchased sixty-four of these flying boats, dubbed 'Small Americas' and they served sufficiently well to begin the British tradition of flying-boat operations which continued unbroken until July, 1957. But at this stage, 1915, they were still being modified by Porte at Felixstowe.

Two other ships, moving nearer to the concept of a flyable aircraft-carrier were afloat in 1915. The *Campania* had a flying-off deck, 120ft long, but it was only occasionally used and never operationally incurring the disdain of Admiral Jellicoe, in whose Grand Fleet she served, on account of her ineffectuality. The other was *Vindex*, another converted Isle of Man packet like *Ben-my-Chree* and she had provision for single-seater fighters to fly off as well as carrying recce aircraft. These were steps forward indeed but in practice they were of little operational effectiveness.

One other incident of 1915 remains to be chronicled, an incident which was a forerunner of later escapades. Intelligence agents had, for some time lost track of the German cruiser *Königsberg* which had been making a nuisance of herself in the Indian Ocean from October, 1914 onwards. Eventually a report came through that she was nestled in the delta of the Rifiji river near Dar-es-Salaam. Eventually these rumours were substantiated by a civilian from South Africa flying a Curtiss flying-boat so the Navy sent some Sopwith seaplanes to follow this news up but they disintegrated in the tropical climate so Short 827's were sent and set up base at Niororo and a landplane base set up on Mafia Island for two Farman and two Caudron landplanes. These were to work in conjunction with the monitors *Severn* and *Mersey*. After that it was only a matter of time and eventually all factors worked well on July 11th with the aircraft spotting for the monitors, their W/T working satisfactorily and in two hours the *Königsberg* was finished. To those close enough to the development of aviation this was one of the many pointers that showed that slowly but surely the RNAS was grappling with the immense problems of applying the somewhat flimsy aviation of the times to the hard taskmaster of war at sea. But to those on the sidelines such progress, if any there was, seemed pitifully slow and there were those who, both within the Royal Navy and without, who were beginning to suspect that the RNAS was an expensive but relatively useless toy. Positive results were needed if public confidence was to be maintained in the Service.

There were straws in the wind already which showed the way ahead and in 1916 some advances were made, notably in the way of equipment. Two more attempts had been made to raid the North German ports by flying off aircraft from seaplane carriers; both *Campania* and *Vindex* had been used and, although they had flying-off decks for'ard these were not used and seaplanes were hoisted overboard to take-off from the open sea. Both attempts were unsuccessful although one did tempt Admiral Scheer to put his fleet to sea. These ignominious raids sealed the fate of the seaplane carrier as such, graphically showing the futility of mounting an operation which relied on flying seaplanes from the open sea. The aircraft-carrier as we know it seemed even farther from fruition than ever as its proponents had to answer for the ineffectuality of these raids and when the only major sea battle of the War took place at Jutland at the end of May, 1916 the only vessel which could have furthered the carrier's cause was *Campania* which, due to a complete muddling over her despatch, left Scapa four hours late. Because she was unescorted and there were U-boats about she was ordered back to Scapa; the only RNAS contingent in the battle being aboard HMS *Engadine* from whom flew Flt Lt Rutland and Asst Paymaster Trewin who made a gallant, low-level recce of the enemy fleet, returning to *Engadine* and putting in a valuable report, earning Rutland the DSC. The irony of the situation however was that, despite frantic efforts, *Engadine* was unable to relay Rutland's information to Admiral Beatty who went into action deprived of the first successful aerial reconnaissance of an enemy fleet. Deterioration of the weather prevented the RNAS from taking any further part in this action.

In February, 1916 the Royal Flying Corps officially took over the responsibility for the air defence of the United Kingdom from the RNAS allowing the latter to concentrate on coastal and North Sea patrols and some advance was to be seen in this field as on April 25th, 1916 when with German warships appearing off Lowestoft, Great Yarmouth Air Station put up a Short piloted by Flt Sub-Lt H. G. Hall who proceeded to bomb the ships although himself wounded. Attempts to increase the range and scope of aircraft over the North Sea led to the attempt to carry aircraft beneath airships; one of Kingsnorth's airships received a BE2c as an appendage, slung beneath its envelope but when the time came to release it tragedy ensued as the aircraft fell prematurely, the pilot being thrown out and the aircraft crashing, killing the other occupant. More orthodox airship operations went well ahead in 1916, further coastal air stations being built to operate them. The SS ships proved most adaptable craft and, with the Navy's forte of improvisation, could suffer what would be considered irreparable damage only to be rebuilt and flown for many a long day. Their more extensive employment drove the U-boats to operate, for their killing, further afield and thus, though the airships saw little in the way of action, they contributed valuably in keeping the submarines below the surface whilst near the British coasts. Production of these craft had gone ahead and the RNAS ended the year with no fewer than 49 SS ships. These were supplemented during the year by a much advanced non-rigid airship, the Coastal class. These ships, which could stay aloft for eleven hours, were of trefoil configuration, having a capacity of 170,000 cu ft and they enabled the airship 'net' to be spread wider than the SS's could manage. The latter were also on the point of being superseded by the SS Zero class, a much improved version of the SS which first went into service from Dunkirk in September, 1916. At this time the RNAS was justifiably putting more faith in lighter-than-air operations as far as North Sea reconnaissance was concerned.

However, it is to the landplanes and the French Front that we look for the positive steps forward in the RNAS. It was here that the Navy's policy of buying from the Aircraft Industry, small though it was at the time, rather than from the official Royal Aircraft Factory at Farnborough bore fruit for from T. O. M. Sopwith's stable in 1916 came two fine fighting aircraft and it was largely the Navy's initiative in ordering them, followed by the War Office deciding that they must have some too, that marked the end of Germany's ascendancy in the air over the British fliers. The first of these was entitled, prosaically enough, the Sopwith Two-Seater, but, due to its w-shaped struts joining the upper wing to the fuselage, was dubbed, and universally known as, the $1\frac{1}{2}$ Strutter. It was first given to the new No 5 Wing which was just being established at Coudekirke in March, 1916 with Caudrons and Farmans. The Sopwiths were to provide fighter escort but in the event the Wing found them a most flexible weapon, flying them as two-seat fighters, single-seat fighters and also as single-seat bombers and by August the Wing was mounting several successful bombing raids in this way. Had the Navy had its way many more $1\frac{1}{2}$ Strutters would have been in operation that summer for No 3 Wing, having returned from the melancholy of the Dardanelles was preparing for the Western Front and was scheduled to use this versatile aircraft to explore the role of strategic bombing (echoes of the early Zeppelin shed raids). But it was the eve of the Battle of the Somme and the RFC was disastrously short of aircraft both numerically and effectively. An appeal was made to the Admiralty, the inter-service hatchet was temporarily buried and most of the RNAS's first $1\frac{1}{2}$ Strutters went into service with the RFC on the Somme.

The other Sopwith design to join the RNAS was a delightful and pretty single-seat scout, acquiring the appropriate name of Pup. The prototype went out in May to 'A' Fighting Squadron at Furness where it was tried out enthusiastically by the pilots. Production aircraft went to No 1 Wing at the end of the summer and the Wing knocked down its first Pup victory in September. With these two aircraft the RNAS was set fair for Western Front activities and in order to give further support to the RFC on the Somme a special Squadron, No 8 (Naval) Squadron was formed which had a flight each of both types and one of Nieuports and which launched into fighting with the RFC. Soon after entering action the Pup was made the sole type used by No 8 and so active was the Squadron that, starting operations in November, had a score of twenty by the end of the year. Thereafter the Pup was thrown into activity with the RFC whose need for a good scout was more pressing than that of the RNAS.

This very disparancy between the two Services in matter of aviation equipment brought to a head an uneasy situation that had been festering for some time, in fact ever since the RFC squadrons took such a hammering at the hands of the Fokker fighter pilots. The success of the $1\frac{1}{2}$ Strutter and Pup gave the impression that the RFC pilots, forced in the main to fly Farnborough-designed aircraft, were in effect fighting with their hands tied behind their backs compared with the RNAS. Action was demanded and Lord Asquith accordingly appointed a committee to co-ordinate supplies and design for the Naval and Military air services. Its chairman, Lord Derby, soon resigned, declaring that there were no division of duties, no principle of co-ordination, his committee had no power or authority and that the Services themselves were completely divided in their outlooks, a sorry condemnation of how far the situation had developed since the Admiralty made its pre-war determination not to be embroiled with the Army but to 'own its own air force'. The collapse of this committee led to the establishment of an Air Board by Lord Curzon with an extension of powers, a Board which clearly looked toward the establishment of a single Air Ministry. Such a threat to its sovereignty was regarded with horror by the Admiralty who openly opposed such an idea but by acting in so obviously partisan a fashion their Lordships could well have hastened the end of the RNAS. It soon became clear that what they were fighting was a rearguard action—the future for British Service Aviation lay with the formation of a single force and slowly but inexorably, hurried along by the more far-seeing officers themselves the organisational aspects of both RNAS and RFC were envisaged as part of a single and separate Service.

But this anticipates events; for many months yet the RNAS continued its paths of development and of action, predominantly wedded to the sea war and to the problems of overcoming the many difficulties of nautical operational flying. Even those units in Northern France which tended to become dragged into the land battle especially when the RFC was hard-pressed were in France primarily for the contribution they could make to the Naval War along the north continental coast both in terms of reconnaissance and, following the Samson tradition, in attack. And it was in the latter role that No 5 Wing now attracts our attention towards the end of 1916 for it is this Wing which operationally developed the long-sighted ideas of that patriarch of British Naval Aviation, Captain Murray Sueter. At the same time that he had launched the seaplane raid on Cuxhaven on Christmas Day 1914 he had issued to a kindred spirit, Mr Frederick Handley Page, an order for a bloody paralyser of an aeroplane for just this role, strategic bombing. Fifth Wing began its raiding with attacks at night by Short 184 seaplanes on Ostend and Zeebrugge. Hazardous enterprises these, for they involved taking-off and landing their flimsy seaplanes from unlit seas but the raids were made although casualties ensued. These seaplanes were used again, even into the Spring of 1917, as part of the offensive against enemy naval installations. Already, however, greater things were in store for at Coudekirke landplane bombers were joining 5 Wing. The first of these were Short Bombers, large 85ft span aircraft powered by one 250 hp Rolls-Royce engines each, able to lift over 500lb of bombs. Going into action first on November 15th in a raid on Ostend they pointed the way ahead although it was plain to see their great disadvantage for the task that was theirs—they only had one engine, thus they were terribly vulnerable to engine failure and to enemy activity. In hot pursuit came Britain's first 'real' bomber, Handley Page's answer to Sueter's request. Designated the 0/100, the first four examples were sent to 5 Wing in November/December, 1916, one of the four overflying Dunkirk and landing in one piece behind the German lines, a most unfortunate start to the aircraft's history but one which it surmounted. To start with these giants of 100ft span with a bomb-load of over 1,700lb were used on coastal patrol up the Belgian coast but in March, 1917 came a solitary raid (there were still only three aircraft in France), but the following month more aircraft enabled both 5 Wing and 3 Wing, which had been formed solely for strategic bombing a year earlier but which had been seriously depleted when aircraft were transferred to the RFC, to begin bombing in earnest.

If 1916 had provided hopeful straws in the wind, promising progress in making aviation a viable tool of the Navy, 1917 was to provide much more substantial evidence that the battle was being won for it was in 1917 that clear lines of progress and of operational activity grew in a heartening way in the Service. One sphere in which progress leapt forward came from Felixstowe. For over a year John Porte had been working hard on the hull problems of the Small America flying-boats, had designed his own giant flying-boat, inevitably dubbed the 'Baby' because of its size, brought into service the Curtiss H12 Large America and, out of the inadequacies of all these boats designed his own 'ideal' flying-boat for coastal patrol, the Felixstowe F2A. The impact of all this activity came in the early summer of 1917 when the Large Americas, modified with armament and Rolls-Royce engines by Porte, came into service over the North Sea. Just in time, too, as it happened, for 1917 was the year of the U-boat and it was against this enemy that the flying-boats were pitted, flying from Yarmouth and Felixstowe on long six to eight hour patrols during which, all too often, nothing but sea was sighted, with ears cocked for the slightest change of engine note which would mean, at best hours afloat on a choppy sea and an intermittent taxying back to East Anglia, at worst a slow and agonizing death from starvation; with eyes skinned for the elusive U-boats, enemy Zeppelins or seaplanes; with bodies aching and frozen by the cold, in conditions which made the World War II Sunderlands and Catalinas seem palatial.

An intricate, but effective system of patrol was worked out which, based on the North Hinder Light Vessel, was flown both by the flying-boats and by the lighter-than-air side of the RNAS and this patrol method, coupled with the recently-introduced convoy system, held the balance in the North Sea battle. Many were the sightings made by the flying-boats, sightings which effectively interrupted the U-boats' activities but of sinkings there were virtually none, only one probable for once again it was discovered that the War at Sea required more than just the application of land battle techniques to the sea; the normal type of bomb, with which the flying-boats were equipped was found to be useless against submarines and the aerial depth charge had not yet been brought into being. For all this, the Large Americas, with their weak hulls and indefensible armament, dicky fuel pumps and primitive crew conditions, became the first effective anti-submarine flying-boats (and indeed fixed-wing aircraft) as they flew their monotonous 'Spider Webs', as their patrols were called, over the North Sea and later over other areas around the UK's coasts. It seems strange today to think that one of the most vital items of equipment carried by these boats was the wicker-basket containing four carrier pigeons which was stowed aboard at the commencement of each flight, to be brought into use when the boat was forced down on the North Sea. These frail means of communications saved the lives of flying-boat crews in the days of 1917. Supplementing these flying-boats were the 'blimps', the non-rigid airships flying from their own Air Stations around the coast; 1917 saw the 'Coastals' supplemented by twelve 'North Seas', a developed trefoil type and by the first of the rigid airships from the operational airship stations at Howden in Yorkshire and Pulham in Norfolk.

It was becoming increasingly clear in the hard school of operational flying that, with the possible exception of the long-range reconnaissance role for which the flying-boat was filling a niche, the only effective fighting aeroplanes were landplanes. The seaplane, unless it could be flown from sheltered waters, was both ineffectual in the air, the drag of its two large floats and the consequent lack of manoeuvrability seeing to this, and too frail on anything but the smoothest of water. So efforts were intensified to solve what appeared to be an intractable problem. With the advantage of hindsight it seems incredible that the flush-deck aircraft-carrier did not spring to mind immediately the problem arose but to understand why, we must attempt to see the situation as it appeared at the time. For three and a half centuries, ever since the days of Drake, the vital factor in naval warfare was the gun. Firepower of the Navy's ships largely dictated ship design, ship tactics and the whole art of naval warfare. And in 1917 this concept was still of prime importance with the Grand Fleet the most important feature of the Royal Navy. True the advent of the submarine, allied to the torpedo, was already challenging this concept but even here this was considered largely in terms of a ship-to-ship problem. The capital ship was very much the ship which could outgun its opponent; into this atmosphere of heavy armour and 18in shells a few enthusiasts, a mere minority within the Navy, had introduced frail flying devices as an addition to the Navy's strength and power but these were seen to be impracticable creatures for war at sea, limiting the Fleet's mobility, and in any event likely to collapse into flotsam when brought into physical contact with the sea itself. And to be fair to the Navy, apart from the shore-based flying-boats the RNAS's activities over the sea had shown little in the first three years of sea warfare to disprove this notion. Small wonder, then that their aircraft were assigned to what were considered little more than auxiliary vessels, floating hangars with engines in. The need for aircraft in a sea battle was little enough recognised, let alone an awareness of the particular type of vessel required by the aviators. Added to which, the RNAS's protagonists were given but junior positions both ashore and afloat and, so often, were their recommendations and expertise countermanded by superiors whose airmindedness was often little greater than the ability to blow up party balloons.

In this context it is not so surprising then that progress had gone little further than the moment when Samson had flown off HMS *Africa* in 1912. Although several of the vessels allotted as aircraft 'carriers' had flying-off decks forward there is little evidence that they were ever used for actual take-offs until Richard Bell-Davies joined *Campania* in 1917 and even then, with seaplanes using jettisonable wheeled trolleys for take-off, these were not used operationally nor did *Campania* launch landplanes on this forward deck.

Instead of seeing the carrier problem as a whole all the development of the time went in the direction of launching aircraft; it was generally the accepted plan that on return the aircraft would ditch, the pilot would be saved and, if there was time, the aircraft recovered. With this notion in mind several blind alleys were followed for a while and because they showed some slight immediate promise probably postponed the day when the planners could be persuaded to talk in terms of what we know as an aircraft-carrier (even though a flush-deck carrier had been suggested before the War and in 1915 detailed proposals were submitted to, and rejected by, the Director of Naval Constructions by a far-seeing H. A. Williamson, ex-*Ark Royal* at Gallipoli). One of these blind alleys was the provision of flying-off platforms on ships of the fleet. These platforms, generally mounted on a forward gun-turret, had the advantage of making no reduction to the vessel's performance and only putting one turret out of action. First such flight was from a platform only twenty feet long, mounted actually on the bows of the cruiser HMS *Yarmouth*; the aircraft was a Pup scout and it was flown by the man who had flown the solitary patrol at the Battle of Jutland the year before, F. J. Rutland. Soon after, a similar flight, only this time in earnest, enabled the pilot, Smart, to attack and destroy the Zeppelin L23; as a result the flying-off platform was seen as an operational step forward and such platforms were in due course installed on over twenty ships.

The other dead end which was explored arose out of a development that John Porte produced at Felixstowe. To increase the range of his flying-boats he built lighters, each one of which took one flying-boat. These were towed across the North Sea behind destroyers at thirty knots or thereabouts after which, if they were still approximately airworthy, they commenced patrolling. As such the lighter formed a rudimentary individual aircraft-carrier; the inventive Samson, having taken over Yarmouth a year later, adapted these for carrying fighters and proceeded to experiment with flying Sopwith Camels from them; as a result of this Lt S. D. Culley rose from one such lighter to destroy Zeppelin L53 in 1918, but this chronologically belongs to our next chapter.

Next step towards the aircraft-carrier came with the commissioning of HMS *Furious* in 1917. She had begun construction as the latest and best of the Navy's 'big guns', literally, for she was to have 18in ones. During construction it was decided to adapt her as the latest aircraft-carrier and when she first appeared she epitomised the crossroads to which the Navy had come; from amidships aft she was the conventional battle-cruiser *par excellence* with her 18in gun turret. But from the bridge for'ard she had an aircraft hangar with a flying-off deck above, and this time it really was a flying-off deck, no 20ft platform but a miniature airfield 228ft long and 50ft wide. At last the Navy had a carrier from which it could launch operational landplanes and its complement was to include Sopwith Pups and 1½ Strutters.

But there were those aboard who saw no reason why they should ditch their aircraft when there was the possibility of landing aboard so trials were instituted for just this purpose. The CO, Sqn Cdr Dunning, began the trials on August 2nd, 1917 whilst the ship was steaming in Scapa Flow. His mount was a Sopwith Pup with toggles under the wings which could be grabbed by personnel on the forward deck to arrest his landing. After his first circuit he approached along the port side and having circumnavigated the funnel and its turbulence, then the Captain in the bridge he sideslipped across, centred over the flight deck almost stationary with an airspeed of upwards of 45 knots and was grabbed out of the air by willing hands and landed. An historic moment indeed. Five days later he tried again, made one landing, went off for a second, was not satisfied with his approach so opened up to go round again, the engine stalled and he went over the side. By the time *Furious* had turned round to pick him up he was drowned. These stirring events had two great effects; first of all the point was made at last that successful carrier operations demanded a landing-on as well as a taking-off and this had been proved possible—just. Secondly, that *Furious* was far too dangerous in her present shape for landing-on operations and the trials were stopped pending her refit during which the 18in gun was removed and aft deck installed; and the new carrier *Argus*, soon to be fitting out was planned at first to have a fore deck and an aft deck with a bridge gantry and then to have a flush deck.

So by the end of 1917 the three main ideas for which the Royal Naval Air Service had striven for so long were now practical possibilities for the immediate future. Already the strategic bomber force, growing out of that wonderful aircraft, the Handley Page, was a practical reality. The first effective anti-submarine reconnaissance, John Porte's Felixstowe F2A, was on the threshold of entering service in considerable numbers and, agonisingly, the true aircraft-carrier, lack of which had halted the progress of truly naval aviation all these years, could now be seen to be on the stocks.

That the RNAS was not to receive the fruits of these endeavours was a bitter pill to swallow. But the ultimate result of the Navy's unilateral action, way back when the Royal Flying Corps was first formed, in not making any attempt to participate was now brought forcibly home. The stirrings of dissatisfaction with our two separate flying services in 1916 we have already mentioned; these continued in the background until the summer of 1917 saw German bomber raids on London which were virtually unopposed and the dissatisfaction rose to public resentment. Britain's air forces were clearly inadequate and ineffective, something must be done. Something was done; a South African General was summoned to sort out the mess into which British military and naval aviation was supposed to have fallen. He came and he acted and the Royal Naval Air Service was lost to the Navy as a result, on the very eve of finding fulfilment in its operational environment.

3

Under New
Management

'You shall go forth yourself . . . as men do who must go into exile.'
(Ezekiel Ch 12)

Whilst the wrangling over aviation matters had been within the offices of
the Service Ministries, obscured under the mask of inter-service intrigue
and jealousy, the dangers and deficiencies of British military aviation were
not widely known; with the undisturbed bombing raids by German Gothas
on London suddenly it was clear to the whole nation that all was far from
well and the need for a wide-ranging investigation into British military
aviation was seen and acted upon. The problem for the Government was to
find a competent military man who was unaffected by loyalties to either
service and the choice fell on the South African General Jan C. Smuts. By
August 17th, 1917 he had formulated his report which was in essence the
answer to three questions:

1. Should there be an 'Air Ministry'?
2. Should there be a single, unified Air Service?
3. How should the relationships between the new Air Service and the
   Army and Navy be regulated?

There is no doubt that, in the long view, Smuts was right in coming down
in favour of a single, unified Air Service with its own ministry; in doing so
he acted with that foresight which was characteristic of the man and as a
result the ensuing Service, the Royal Air Force, was ahead of the World in
constitution and thinking both at its inception and down the years. Unfortunately, he paid little more than lip-service to the third question,
leaving running sores in the corridors of the Admiralty, War Office and the
new Air Ministry which engendered much negative activity and energy
over the ensuing years and hindered full development of naval aviation
for far too long.

With fifty years' hindsight it is easy to see the weaknesses but it must be
remembered that the climate of thought in those days was very different to
that of today. The majority of military experts were only just beginning to

see that the aircraft was useful for much more than reconnaissance, the enthusiastic exponents of air power were claiming exaggerated capabilities for it, capabilities which were only practical two or three decades later. The arguments put forward by the older service representatives were to some extent suspect due to their own loyalties and prejudices whilst the views put forward by the proponents of a separate air service were clear, fresh, logical and very convincing. Had it been realised that both the Army and the Navy needed their own air arms in addition to an independent air force years of bitter controversy could have been saved but such an awareness came much later.

Smuts' report was accepted and the target date for the creation of the unified service was, to many, an appropriate one—April 1st, 1918 (All Fools' Day). When the day came the two services involved, the Royal Flying Corps and the Royal Naval Air Service, were desperately involved in driving back the German armies in France, in combating the U-boat menace in the North Sea and the Atlantic and in the various other campaigns in the Mediterranean and Africa into which the War had proliferated. To the men on active service the change-over was to a large extent incidental to the main purpose of getting on with the War and, with the British trait of being able to get on with the job in hand, the operational side of the change was minimal. True the naval gentlemen had to become accustomed to the indignity of Army ranks and the RNAS units were all renumbered so that the incomparable 'Naval Eight' (No 8 Squadron, RNAS) was now cloaked by the anonymity of No 208 Squadron, RAF but the units were the same units, the men and machines were the same and so was the enemy to be fought. So until the end of the War the bitterness of the changeover was only apparent in the offices of Whitehall. Its effects after the War bit much deeper.

But for the moment there was much to be done, not least of which was the winning of a war. In this the naval aviators, now 'airmen' in the Royal Air Force, continued along the lines they were already pursuing. The scout squadrons in France, now largely re-equipped with the splendid Sopwith Camel, were caught up in the crescendo of the immense dogfights of the Spring and Summer of 1918 and then in the final offensive. It fell to one of these squadrons, No 209, to expunge that most famous of all the German aces, von Richthofen, when Capt Roy Brown shot him down on April 21st, 1918. During this final six months of fighting these squadrons were fully committed to the land battle alongside their erstwhile RFC companions. The heavy bomber squadrons, too, had become part of the Independent Air Force and flew their strategic sorties well behind the lines carrying out the dictums laid down by Murray Sueter years before. In the more naval aspects of aviation 1918 was an interesting year in that many of the developments which had been groped towards down the years at last came to fruition. It was under the aegis of the RAF that the growth of the coastal patrol set-up blossomed into a practicality with bases both for land and sea planes all around the coasts of the UK, no fewer than 78 of them. From these flew the non-rigid airships, a variety of landplanes and the flying-boats. The latter had really come to the fore under the guidance of John Porte and those which flew out over the North Sea from Yarmouth and Felixstowe now flew in formation, ready to tangle with the seaplanes from Ostend, Zeebrugge, Borkum and Nordeney. Their patrols were backed up by DH4s and DH9s with a fighter escort of Camels, a long cry from the futile attempts of Sopwith Schneider seaplanes of three years previously. At last it was evident that the flyingboat was a better proposition than the seaplane and during the year the Short seaplanes were being phased out as quickly as possible, for open sea work, by the Felixstowe flying-boats which had reached a stage at which they were a viable proposition. The only fly in the North Sea ointment was the DH9 whose engine was notoriously unreliable. Away from the active fighting area of the North Sea the coastal flights were less belligerent, being formed generally for the purpose of discovering enemy vessels with a view to directing surface vessels to the spot. For this task a variety of aircraft were employed, chief amongst them being the hideous DH6. By a stretch of imagination one could conceive this as Geoffrey de Havilland's first attempt at a Tiger Moth, being a training biplane built in the simplest way; thus the fuselage resembled a coffin and the wings were planklike and mounted with slight back-stagger whilst the engine up front had two tall chimneys to carry the exhaust above the top wing. This aircraft presented an appearance to earn it nicknames such as 'The Clutching Hand' or 'The Flying Coffin' but it had the advantages of inherent stability and slow-flying characteristics to enable it to find and stay with surface and underwater vessels and summon naval assistance. Being ousted from the Training Squadrons by the more lively Avro 504 trainer, the DH6 was available in numbers and found a useful occupation flying coastal patrols from impossibly small fields on cliffs around the country.

It was in 1918, however, that the biggest of all naval aviation's problems found a solution in a form which has since become classic. Following the paradoxically successful disaster of Cdr Dunning's landing aboard HMS *Furious* with a Sopwith Pup the concept of a flush-deck carrier, propounded on several occasions in the past by far-seeing but junior officers, now was clearly the only possible solution to the successful launching and recovery of aircraft at sea. This had been decided upon when the final configuration of the *Argus* was hammered out during construction. Starting life as an Italian liner, the *Conte Rosso*, she was taken over early on to be the Navy's new aircraft carrier. For a long time she was envisaged as having two flying decks, one forward for launching, one aft for recovery, with the superstructure in between, but experience with the *Furious* convinced all concerned that landing behind a superstructure was just too turbulent to be on. So they went the whole hog on the *Argus* and built her with a completely flush deck, the exhaust being carried to the stern and discharged there. She was immediately dubbed 'The Flat-Iron' for obvious reasons, her utility being more noticeable than her grace of line. She was to commission in October, 1918, too late to play any part in the War. Working up for her was the answer to another of the Navy's problems, a squadron of Sopwith Cuckoo torpedo-bombers. *Argus* formed the basis on which all the problems of realistic carrier operation could be evolved and certainly earned her keep for the Navy; she was still in use in World War II as a training carrier, accepting on her deck aircraft at landing speeds undreamt of when she commissioned.

With the signing of the Armistice in November, 1918 the War to end all wars was over. During it Aviation had grown up from a plaything to a useful tool and already held promise of becoming a tyranny in the hands of wicked men. For the Navy's aeronautical protagonists it had been a war of constantly trying to do the impossible by applying such aerial tools as it could obtain or adapt to the very difficult problems of naval warfare. Slowly, but slowly, these difficulties were overcome or brought within reach of taming but the fruition came at last within an organisational framework distasteful to the Navy itself, a new and untried management.

This very creation posed a heartsearching decision for the members of the Royal Naval Air Service for they were given the option of transfer to the Royal Air Force or a return to a normal career in the Navy itself. The RNAS had perforce grown into a body of men who, because they were a minority of enthusiasts in a Service which, to a large extent, disbelieved in their efficacy, had become passionate devotees of flying and keenly embued with a determination to prove that naval flying could work and had a future. To ask such men to give up flying and return to the surface-bound Navy was too much for most of them and so, to the Navy's misfortune subsequently, the great majority of the practising aviators left the Navy's ranks to further naval flying as part of the Royal Air Force. This left the Navy itself devoid of a body of practised and experienced naval aviators to advise and guide in the future.

The new Service, scarcely a year old, was faced with an early crisis in its career when peacetime reductions called upon in 1919 reduced its strength from upwards of two hundred squadrons to twenty-five and the two older services, and principally the Navy, pressed hard for the dissolution of the RAF and its return, piecemeal, to its originators. It was in the main Trenchard's stubborn insistence on 'The Unity of the Air' which alone held out against their onslaught but the first half of the 'twenties saw much infighting within the ministries and inside Parliament between those with various service loyalties, some of which was hardly of credit either to the Services or to Parliament. Much of it need not be recorded here and in any case much is better left in the limbo of the past, the positive action that took place being the establishment of the Balfour Committee in 1923 to investigate this whole problem of the control and working of Fleet Air Work. To this Committee came Beatty and Trenchard, with their lesser minions, and thundered the one at the other before the Committee which drew up its report for reading immediately before the end of the summer recess of Parliament. By a stroke of fortune (ill or good according to one's viewpoint) when Parliament re-assembled it was to be dissolved and the new Government had weightier problems on its hands than to consider a six-month old report. Thus its recommendations were carried out without any debate whatsoever. And its recommendations were firmly in support of the status quo for control, although making concessions to Beatty on certain operational aspects. That this was much less than satisfactory became evident down the years for the Navy never ceased its battle for complete control, a measure which it eventually regained at the worst possible moment.

In the meantime, what was happening at the 'sharp end'? With the formation of the Royal Air Force both the strategic bombing force and the coastal patrol force which had been pioneered by the Naval fliers became so much part of the new service as to be largely divorced from naval aviation. The Independent Air Force was now reduced to a small Command, with its headquarters on that home of the Army, Salisbury Plain, and designated 'Bombing Area'. Likewise the coastal bases became 'Coastal Area' and concentrated on the building up of a small fleet of flying-boats which emerged eventually as Coastal Command just before World War II. However, it was in Coastal Area that the remannts of truly naval flying were operating. These were now all concerned with aeroplanes for the lighter-than-air fleet vanished almost overnight apart from a small development contingent that soldiered on with the Royal Air Force, though not for naval purposes.

When the cuts had taken place after the Armistice the Navy possessed the flush-deck carrier HMS *Argus* together with various seaplane carriers, one spotter-reconnaissance squadron, half a torpedo squadron and a fighter flight for service aboard *Argus* together with a seaplane flight and a flying-boat flight. These, apart from the torpedo flight which had Sopwith Cuckoos, were equipped with wartime aircraft. The flying units were under the control of the RAF who manned them and serviced them, ashore and afloat. Whilst they were afloat they came under naval orders as regards operational use, whereas the ships themselves were entirely naval. Of course this posed its problems but it has always been remarkable how, when put to it, the British serviceman drops even service barriers when there is a job to do and there was certainly this for here was the first flush-deck carrier, a fleet of aircraft designed to operate from grass fields and the need to evolve a system of operating these from the carrier safely and effectively in a fighting role.

Almost immediately the first attempts to provide aircraft specifically for carrier operation appeared. One of the problems of divorcing practical aviators from the Admiralty now arose, for the specifications which evolved required too much from the poor aircraft designer and there began a series of aircraft in service with the Fleet, especially in the TSR (Torpedo Spotter Reconnaissance) role which varied from the unlovely to almost the impossible in appearance. First of these to join the Sopwith Cuckoo for service aboard *Argus* were the Parnall Panther which resembled a Sopwith Camel with an even more humped and rotund fuselage and two seats but which had a folding fuselage to fit the cramped space aboard a carrier; and the Westland Walrus, a type of DH9a with what looked like duck's disease and which laboured under the disadvantage of having to use up surplus DH9a wings and tailplane. They were joined in 1922 by the Nieuport Nightjar, a specifically carrier fighter evolved from the Nieuport Nighthawk and built by what became the Gloster Aircraft Co.

With these and older, wartime, types the *Argus* was used to experiment with various means of efficient operation. The main problem was landing the aircraft safely. Left to their own and the pilot's devices the tendency was for the aircraft to slide gaily along the flight deck and on over the bows or, alternatively, to drop off the sides into the sea. So some form of arresting was necessary and for a considerable time the early carriers carried length-wise wires spaced about nine inches apart and devices were fixed to the axles of the aircraft which would engage these wires and, in theory, keep the aircraft running straight, at the same time decelerating it. This was the basic system but there were refinements and additions. Whether by design or accident it is not recorded but on one occasion a landing was made with the forward lift a few inches below deck level, the aircraft dropping on to the lift and slowing immediately, an advantageous effect which was continued. A system of ramps, up which the aircraft ran and dropped into a trap of fore-and-aft wires slowing it down until a final ramp brought it to a halt. This was refined on HMS *Eagle* with the wires mounted on hinged flaps which the aircraft knocked flat on landing, dissipating its momentum. All of these were tried but the system of longitudinal wires was basically at fault for if the aircraft landing had any drift component on at all it was almost certain to be tipped on its nose or wingtip by the wires fouling its progress, and a period ensued in which most aircraft landed freely, without any means of deceleration other than the pilot's skill.

However, the concept of the flush-deck carrier had been proved and further carriers were quickly on the way. *Furious* had been taken back into

Rosyth and later Devonport dockyards and emerged with a completely flush deck surmounted on the ship's hangar, the forward end of which opened out on to a lower fore-deck from which fighter aircraft could take-off, a deck which was used until just before World War II. To join these two came two further carriers, HMS *Eagle* stemming from a projected Chilean dreadnought *Almirante Cochrane* which was never completed. She appeared in the summer of 1920 and went back for modifications, finally joining the fleet early in 1924; she had a large superstructure on the starboard side with, eventually, two funnels. Contemporary with *Eagle* was HMS *Hermes*, the first carrier laid down as such, and following the same layout as *Eagle* but with one funnel.

The Balfour Committee, whilst largely endorsing Trenchard's views, had opened up certain avenues for the Navy. One of these was the recognition of something which the Navy had instituted some three years before, the establishment of naval observers for flying duties and it was agreed that all the 'back-seat drivers' should be naval officers. The Committee's recommendations were that not less than 30 per cent of pilots should be Air Force officers which was interpreted that 70 per cent of the pilots should be naval officers, by the Navy at least. On these twin bases the Navy began to build up a nucleus of flying personnel for the years ahead. In time these were to make up for the exodus of practising aviators to the RAF when it was first formed but the effect was not to be felt for a decade or two.

In the meantime the Fleet Air Arm of the Royal Air Force, as it was now officially designated, began to receive a generation of aircraft one stage beyond wartime designs, or adaptations thereof, a generation in answer to the requirements of naval planners. Easiest of the specifications to meet was the fleet fighter requirement which produced one of the classic aircraft of the inter-war years, the Fairey Flycatcher. This dimunitive and dainty aircraft was beloved by all who flew it and many others besides for it was strong, a delight to fly, and fitted in to fleet work aboard carriers and capital ships from the start. It was equipped with either floats or wheels and flew both from carriers and from the catapults of battleships and cruisers. It first entered service with 402 Flight in 1923, going aboard HMS *Eagle* in 1924 and remained in first-line service for eight years. Alongside the Fly-catcher, but in the Fleet Spotter Reconnaissance role was another aircraft from the Fairey stable. It progressed from the Fairey III Series seaplanes of immediately after the War and entered full-scale service as the IIID in 1922 and the later IIIF which remained in first-line service until 1933. The IIIF was the 'maid-of-all-work' in the Fleet Air Arm for a whole decade (as well as serving with the land-based RAF) and, with floats or wheels, operated from ships and airfields on a multitude of tasks. The third type required was to fulfill the Torpedo Bomber Reconnaissance role and this fell to a Blackburn design, the Dart. A large, single-seat, heavy torpedo bomber it was, however, just what the Fleet needed at the time to perfect its torpedo techniques for it was sturdy and relatively easy to fly and operate from carriers. With these three types the Fleet Air Arm grew out of the era when its aircraft were either left-offs from the First War or improbable-looking devices such as the Avro Bison and Blackburn Blackburn.

As hinted already, a further development that had been taking place had been the installation of catapults aboard the battleships and many of the cruisers. It was inevitable that the gun-platform which had served for the taking-off of Sopwith $1\frac{1}{2}$ Strutters and Pups would not suffice the newer aircraft and anyway it had never been popular with that influential Admiralty lobby, the Gunnery Officers. So catapults were installed and each ship given its own spotter aircraft, more often than not the ubiquitous IIIF. Such development stood the test of time and in the second conflict the catapult ships used their aircraft to great effect—until the aircraft-carrier at length superseded the battleship.

It was in 1926 that the Fleet Air Arm of the Royal Air Force made the first of what was to become a typical operation in the years ahead and one that was indicative of the need for an ever-present carrier force for preserving peace, a need that has certainly not dwindled with time even though the carrier force has. In that year the bandits of China were interfering with British commerce both ashore and afloat at Hong Kong and Shanghai and a carrier force was, for the first time, despatched to keep the peace. *Hermes* went to Hong Kong and there, with her aircraft equipped with floats, flew them from the harbour on anti-bandit patrols. To Shanghai went *Argus* and her aircraft were flown ashore to the racecourse from where they too operated. Those in the carriers were quick to realise the potential of this type of mobility but it is doubtful whether such faraway happenings even rippled the waters of Whitehall. Of more significance was a similar happening two years later when HMS *Courageous*, newest and grandest of the Fleet's aircraft carriers and therefore in the limelight, moved from Malta to Jaffa with all her aircraft and a battalion of troops with their transport and equipment, ready to deal with a Jewish/Arab flare-up within three days of the call.

Courageous was important to the Fleet Air Arm in another way for it was aboard this ship that the answer was eventually found to the question of arresting aircraft on landing. With the three aircraft mentioned above the flying characteristics were such as to enable the normally-skilled service pilot to land without any form of arresting and having some certainty that he would come to a halt on the deck with his aircraft unscathed. But naturally a means of arresting this and newer generations of aircraft would be advantageous so *Courageous* was fitted, in 1928, with wires transverse to the aft deck and a hook placed under the rear fuselage of the aircraft which would engage the wire and pull the aircraft to an abrupt halt.

Experiments were encouraging and the wires were linked to winches to provide a smooth deceleration; however, these tended to pull the aircraft to one side or another and the real answer was found, aboard *Courageous*, in 1933 when the same system of wires was linked to hydraulic cylinders which allowed a smooth, balanced pull-out, a system which has stood the test of higher speeds and greater weights up to this present day. By then *Courageous* had been joined by her sister ship *Glorious* which first commissioned in 1930 and the Fleet had a large peacetime force of carriers.

After ten years of joint RAF/Navy administration the pundits could look at the Fleet Air Arm and say with some justification that all was substantially well. The main imponderables that were on the point of solving when the RNAS was overwhelmed in 1918 had largely been overcome, Britain had a carrier force of some magnitude including two reasonably modern ships, solutions had been found to the problems of deck operation and the two services involved were working together in reasonable accord, at least at flight-deck level. Only when those involved cast their eyes at two navies which had control over their own air arms, the Japanese and the Americans, could they see what they fancied they had lost by losing naval independence for, by comparison with both these navies, the Fleet Air Arm was small and ill-equipped and mounted upon obsolescing carriers. And so, deep down within the Navy, the determination to possess its own aviation remained as inexorable as ever.

Meanwhile with the coming of the 'thirties came welcome new aircraft. That remarkable fighter of the Royal Air Force, the Fury, had been navalised as the Nimrod and entered the carrier hangars in company with a two-seat fighter version of the Hawker Hart, named the Osprey in 1932. Thus the fighter flights now acquired some observers in their aircraft assisting in the overwater navigation; the IIIF began to be replaced by a re-vamped, radial-engined version called the Fairey Seal and the Dart gave way to the Blackburn Ripon and later Baffin. Another innovation, now that aircraft were becoming heavier, was the introduction to aircraft carriers of the highly successful catapults which were throwing IIIFs, Seals and Ospreys into the air from battleships and cruisers with great aplomb. On the carriers they were known as 'accelerators' and were fitted near the bows to facilitate deck operations generally.

In 1933 the Flights, which formed the standard formations on board the carriers were augmented and re-classified as squadrons to provide a better operational system and, because they were under RAF control, they were given new squadron numbers in the eight-hundred series, with fighter squadrons in the eight-hundreds, FSR squadrons in the eight-hundred and tens and TBR squadrons in the eight-hundred and twenties. Second-line units were numbered in the seven-hundreds. Thus were born some of the familiar FAA squadron numbers which attained fame in the years ahead.

By now, too, the units had already been painting their aircraft with distinguishing markings. Each carrier used a different colour and all its aircraft carried markings in that colour (eg *Courageous*-red; *Glorious*-yellow; *Furious*-blue; *Eagle*-green; *Hermes*-black). Furthermore, the fighter squadrons especially adapted these colours to provide, not simply the standard fuselage band in that colour, but coloured bars and other devices across the upper wing, rivalling in gaiety the RAF's land-based fighter squadrons. Of such stuff was the peacetime air and deportment of the Fleet Air Arm of the Royal Air Force!

But as the 'thirties wore on so, belatedly, came the awareness that all was not peaceful in the contemporary Europe and that twin and fearsome heads of belligerence were rearing up, threatening to engulf neighbours near and far. Sleeping Albion awakened in haste and began to prepare for a possible conflict once more and in the scramble to modernise its military aviation the worst fears of the Admirals, that any naval branch of the RAF would fare badly in terms of equipment and attention, began to be realised. To face the situation one new carrier, *Ark Royal* was laid down and for aircraft the only solid prospect on the horizon was a new all-purpose biplane designed to combine the FSR and TBR roles and designated TSR. Two types competed for this task and small batches of both the Blackburn Shark and the Fairey Swordfish were built for evaluation and service and the performance of the Shark outstripped the Swordfish. Not surprisingly, the Shark was relegated to the training role and the Swordfish went on to become one of the world's great aeroplanes, the crowing indignity being that most of the wartime Swordfishes were built by Blackburns.

Faced with a massive German Luftwaffe the Royal Air Force was now preoccupied with intensive activity to build up a strong bomber and fighter force to meet what was clearly going to be predominantly an air war when it came. Understandably, it could give little time to modernising what was considered to be a force for the protection of shipping in an area where little or no air opposition would be encountered—surely old biplanes on old ships would be sufficient to deal with enemy shipping, capital ships and U-boats alike for the probable protagonists had no carriers at all?

Such obvious neglect became of major concern to many in the Navy and to one man in particular, Admiral Chatfield, First Sea Lord, in 1935. He had been working towards the resumption of naval control inexorably and it was in that year that he was instrumental in launching again the campaign for naval control once more, envisaging the take-over, not only of the seaborne air force but of the Coastal Area, or Coastal Command as it was now known, as well. Despite several rebuffs Chatfield was eventually able to persuade Sir Thomas Inskip, Minister for the Co-ordination of Defence, to form a committee to look into this whole question once more. The Committee, though ostensibly three men, was in practice but one, Sir

Thomas Inskip himself, for the other two, Lord Halifax and Oliver Stanley, played little or no part in it; Inskip was a lawyer by training and this enabled him to form a concise summing-up of the situation with the result that his vital recommendations were to remove the Fleet Air Arm from the Royal Air Force and give it control over its own organisation, training and equipment but to leave Coastal Command with the Royal Air Force, a decision which meant that, to all intents and purposes, the long battle was over; the Navy could now once again own its own air force.

For all this satisfaction the Navy now had a man-size task on its hands. At a time of rapid, almost panic, expansion it had now to build its own air service, virtually from scratch, competing with the RAF, for personnel and equipment. But the will to make it work was there and furious activity ensued. Four shore airfields were handed over by the RAF, Donibristle, Gosport, Lee-on-Solent and Worthy Down, for training and work-up bases and a headquarters. Pilot training, it was agreed, would remain in the hands of the RAF, but no longer would thirty per cent of the pilots in the Fleet Air Arm be in light blue—all would be naval. There were some new aircraft on the brink of service but here again the years had brought a tacit assumption that naval aircraft inevitably had to be down on performance compared with their landbased counterparts and all except one of those types on the brink of service were soon eclipsed in the hard schooling of war. That exception was the Walrus, an amphibian flying-boat which took over the catapults of the non-carrier ships and earned itself a fascinating place in war-time history as we shall see. For its new fighter the Navy was about to receive the Sea Gladiator, a navalised version of the biplane which was already seen to be outmoded in the RAF (this at a time when the US Navy had plans for two monoplane fighters, the F2A and the F4F). One monoplane was on order, the Blackburn Skua dive-bomber which in the event flew some useful sorties in the opening rounds of the War and until better aircraft appeared but was too dainty an aircraft for the rigours of naval warfare; its counterpart, the Roc fighter, was encumbered with a four-gun turret which was too heavy to enable it to behave as a fighter. To supplement the Swordfish was an up-dated sophisticated version, the Albacore which in the event was outlived by the Swordfish itself.

Intense activity, recruiting, planning, organising, training, purchasing, marked what was but a few months before the Navy, with its own Air Branch once more, was launched into the bitter testing of World War II.

4

Taking the Strain

'Behold I send you out as sheep in the midst of wolves' (St Matthew Ch 10)

Had they known the amount of time that was theirs to rebuild a naval air service before being plunged into the new World Conflict their Lordships might not have been so enthusiastic about resuming control of the Fleet Air Arm which they now succinctly entitled 'The Air Branch', a name which meant little to anyone outside the Service, it still being popularly referred to as the Fleet Air Arm. However activity was prodigious on all fronts and when September 3rd, 1939 brought renewed hostilities against an old enemy the Fleet Air Arm was a going concern even if ill-equipped and smaller than was necessary.

Even so, it was a shaky and unnerving beginning for the Fleet Air Arm. The three carriers in home waters were immediately put on to anti-submarine patrol in the Western Approaches to the Atlantic, each carrier having a protecting destroyer screen. Within a fortnight it was seen how unready the Fleet Air Arm was for *Ark Royal* was attacked by a U-boat and all but torpedoed; three days later another U-boat evaded *Courageous*'s patrolling Swordfish, sank the carrier, and escaped in safety. Clearly risks like these would soon reduce the carrier force to nil so they were regrouped into raider hunting groups with other warships. Whilst these groups were largely looking for surface raiders they had the advantage of keeping any U-boats in the vicinity well down. In the course of this *Ark Royal*'s Skuas claimed the first German aircraft shot down in World War II, a Dornier Do 18 flying boat.

Only one of these hunter groups, Force K with *Ark Royal*, had any success, capturing the German *Uhenfels* and also staying in the background of the *Admiral Graf Spee* episode. This latter brought into action the catapult aircraft of the Fleet Air Arm, carried aboard battleships and cruisers. This action, fought out by cruisers, involved the Fairey Seafox, a light reconnaissance seaplane chiefly remembered for giving the observer a cosy, enclosed cabin and leaving the pilot out in the cold. Two were aboard HMS *Ajax* and one of these maintained a spotting service for the cruisers' guns throughout the action. HMS *Exeter*'s two Walrus had been put out of action and *Achilles* Walrus had been left ashore. Whilst these few actions were providing some hard fighting the rest of the Fleet Air Arm was gaining precious time to consolidate its organisation and to get in much practice flying in the rigours of winter weather. This especially applied to the squadrons afloat on the carriers for whom the winter Atlantic was something of a new experience.

It was not until April, 1940 that the Fleet Air Arm was extensively engaged in action and in a way which had been part of Naval Aviation's earliest activities and has remained so until recent times. As usual, the Navy was not well placed to cope with the threat but cope it did. From a guarded neutrality Norway had been thrown into action by the depradations of Hitler and the duplicity of Quisling. The Navy was quick to react and hastily cut short the refit of HMS *Furious* sending her across the North Sea in such haste as to leave behind her fighter squadron, an act showing little regard for the realities of the situation. To remedy this situation were the Skuas of *Ark Royal* which were ashore at Hatston in the Orkneys. These attacked the cruiser *Königsberg* at Bergen and sank her whilst *Furious* Swordfish made torpedo attacks at Trondheim. The Walrus squadron, also at Hatston, flew their aircraft on long reconnaissance patrols to Norway with some success. *Ark Royal* and *Glorious* (from the Mediterranean) arrived to relieve *Furious*, damaged by near-misses and now they could provide some semblance of fighter cover for the Army ashore although the aircraft used, Sea Gladiators from *Glorious* and Skuas from *Ark Royal*, were both slower than one of their principal protagonists, the Junkers Ju88. *Glorious*, in addition, put ashore a squadron of RAF Gladiators which, for a brief two days, flew fighter patrols until they had been put out of action. *Glorious* and *Furious* then brought more Gladiators and Hurricanes to Norway—it was ironical that the RAF Hurricane Squadron (No. 46) flew off and subsequently landed on *Glorious* without previous deck-landing training despite the pundits having said that the Hurricane was too potent to be used by carriers. The Walrus unit from Scapa now had a base at Harstadt from where its six amphibians gave themselves unstintingly until forced out, whereupon they embarked upon *Ark Royal* for the return home. With the Norwegian campaign collapsing *Glorious* went in to recover the RAF Gladiators and Hurricanes. Having them safely aboard she and her destroyer screen ran into the *Scharnhorst* and *Gneisenau* and were summarily despatched to the bottom of the North Sea with fearful loss of life. The Royal Navy was learning the hard way the abilities and limitations of aircraft carriers.

This was June, 1940, the month when France collapsed and Italy entered the War and when aircraft production in the UK was concentrated on fighters for the forthcoming Battle of Britain. Clearly the Fleet Air Arm could not expect anything miraculous in the way of new equipment although longing eyes were cast at the US Navy's prospective monoplanes, longings which became facts later on. To replace the two carriers lost were two more all but complete and these were to a new and more advanced design, a design in which the priority was given to invulnerability. Even the complement of aircraft to be carried was reduced in order to make the carriers unsinkable and this philosophy paid handsome dividends for although five of the six ships of this class were all hit at one time or another, and on occasion hit so heavily that other carriers would have been sunk, not one of them was lost and on several occasions they were back in action after a remarkably short time. These vessels formed the *Illustrious* class and made a great contribution to the Fleet Air Arm's war, the first vessel *Illustrious* becoming operational in August, 1940 and *Formidable* in November. But before these could make their mark the situation was tenuous—*Furious* was repairing from her Norwegian punishment, *Ark Royal* went south to form part of the famous Force H hunter/killer group, *Eagle* was en route for the Mediterranean after a lengthy refit in Singapore and *Hermes* was still part of a group in the South Atlantic which now had the additional role of bottling up the French fleet at Dakar.

There remained one carrier, the daddy of them all, *Argus* which had long since been relegated to training duties. She was in the Mediterranean providing deck-landing training from the French base of Hyeres using the Swordfish crews off *Courageous* as instructors in her training squadron No 767. Of course she had to leave Hyeres and, with typical naval aplomb her training squadron decided to have a go at Italy on the way. Accordingly they bombed up the Swordfish and set out for Genoa, providing one of the early bombing raids on Italian soil. Having alarmed the Genoese they flew on to Malta to land. Their arrival there was fortuitous because a bombing and torpedo force on that island could be put to good use. The Squadron was re-organised and renumbered (No 830 Squadron) and began a task which was carried through most successfully for nearly three years. Malta was nicely placed to 'supervise' the continual stream of supply ships running between Italy and its North African possessions and 830 quickly developed an expertise of dealing with such ships with bomb and torpedo, by day and eventually by night also. The Squadron continued on this task, augmented at times by other squadrons with Albacores, the 'pullman' development of the Swordfish, until there was no further cause for Italian ships to sail to Africa, in which time a prodigious amount of shipping had been sunk.

After the disasters early in the War when carriers were put on anti-submarine duties it was not seen fit to return them to these duties and so *Ark Royal* took her place in Force H, *Eagle* joined the Eastern Med fleet and *Furious* and *Argus* became largely ferry carriers for a while, ferrying aircraft to West Africa to be flown across to Egypt. Whilst on these duties they encountered the *Admiral Hipper* but were unable to put any aircraft into the action before the German raider was driven off. It was clear that the Mediterranean was to be the cockpit for the Fleet Air Arm's fighting in the near future—*Ark Royal* was at the western end, *Eagle* at the eastern and here she was joined by the newest of the new, *Illustrious* herself bringing to the scene a new fighter, the Fairey Fulmar. To be sure it was a monoplane and it did carry eight .303 machine-guns wing-mounted but it lacked that one essential of the fighter, speed, its maximum being 280mph. However for the task in hand in the Mediterranean it was deemed suitable, and in fact to start with it maintained air superiority over the British fleets in the Mediterranean with considerable success.

Eagle and *Illustrious* were soon put to offensive work in this area against Italian ports, forcing them to relinquish some of their North African ports for anything but the smallest of vessels; and against Italian shipping which ventured forth at considerable risk. The juiciest target for the Navy, however, was the Italian battle fleet which needed dealing with to ensure that British merchantmen could go about their business unhindered. As the Italians would not come out and fight for *Mare Nostrum* it was intended to take the fight to them. Originally chosen for Trafalgar Day the attack took place eventually on November 11th, 1940 and it must have been an eye-opener to those naval officers who still, in that day and age, could see little use for the Fleet Air Arm. The attack was carried out on the fleet at Taranto by twenty-one Swordfish flying from *Illustrious*, of which six aircraft were from *Eagle*'s squadrons. By combining a dive-bombing attack with a torpedo attack the enemy defences, which were alert and ready, were confused and major damage was accomplished by the two waves of aircraft. As well as crippling the major portion of the Italian Fleet the Swordfish put out of action the Taranto seaplane base, thus blinding the Italian Navy's eyes considerably. Two Swordfish were lost and one crew killed; scarcely can there have been greater value for money. But the effect of this attack was greater than just the damage, considerable though that was for once and for all the offensive value of carrier-based strike aircraft had been proved, no longer could carrier-based aircraft be relegated to a minor place in the scheme of naval war. The Italians, poor souls, took such fright that, when two weeks later the remainder of their fleet was in a tactically good position to attack the British fleet off Spartivento the mere appearance of *Ark Royal*'s aircraft caused them to turn and run; it was also evident, a year later at Pearl Harbour, that the Japanese had learnt the lesson that Taranto taught.

But soon a formidable new foe entered the Mediterranean. Germany had long felt that she would have to come to the assistance of her partner and now that most of Europe was subdued and the invasion of Britain postponed a Luftwaffe Fliegerkorps was spared for the Mediterranean; a specialist in anti-shipping work it soon altered the picture in the inland sea as did the Afrika Korps in North Africa. Based in Sicily the Germans had an immediate success on January 10th, 1941 when they caught *Illustrious* off Malta and gave her such a pounding as would have expunged any normal ship. She lurched into Malta, where she was again bombed and after jury repairs set sail for the United States, for a rebuilding which took the rest of that year.

However the second of her class, *Formidable*, had already been at sea in the South Atlantic and by April had been brought round to the Suez Canal where she came, with one squadron of Fulmars and two of Albacores, to relieve the tired, old *Eagle* which, unarmoured and slow had a small complement of aircraft that was more a liability than an asset in the new situation in the Mediterranean. *Formidable* had been an Atlantic ship and her removal left *Hermes*, plus *Ark Royal* with Force H as the only carriers to cover North and South Atlantic. However, *Hermes* moved to the Indian Ocean in February, 1941 and was eventually followed by *Albatross*, a seaplane carrier which had been stationed off West Africa as a radio link with East Africa and also to provide some sort of shipping patrol over the area with 710 Squadron's Walrus amphibians. These gallant jack-of-all-trades aircraft performed a multitude of tasks and although cast in a passive role, such was the individuality of their crews and the opportunities for lone action that on not a few occasions in trouble spots around the world these "Shagboats" as they were called were to be seen in most improbable poses dive-bombing some shipping in an obscure Italian port or darting around enemy shipping spotting for the guns of its parent ship.

The departure of *Hermes* and *Albatross* to the east left but one carrier in the Atlantic, *Ark Royal*, and she committed to the activities of Force H. This had already involved the melancholy task of putting the French fleet out of action at Oran and Dakar, a job originally shared with *Hermes*. She had also been involved in the occasional convoy to Malta, livening these up with strikes against Italian land bases within range. One of these was flown as a diversion to enable the crippled *Illustrious* to make through the Sicilian Narrows to Alexandria. This attack on the *Illustrious* had changed the face of Mediterranean operations making convoys, or indeed any shipping activity, in the regions of Malta both unhealthy and potentially costly. After a quick refit in the UK, during which she replaced her Skuas with a squadron of Fulmars, *Ark Royal* returned to Force H and whilst thus occupied was drawn into the chase of the *Bismarck*. In this she was preceded by another carrier, the very new *Victorious*; it was May 22nd and this newly-commissioned ship lay at Scapa with the Home Fleet, intending to make her first voyage a ferry one to West Africa with Hurricanes for the RAF. Accordingly her own aircraft fleet was reduced to nine Swordfish and six Fulmars. The full details of this memorable action are too well known and too complicated to repeat here but it is of value to see how the FAA elements took part. It was a Walrus from the cruiser *Norfolk* which shadowed the German ship for nearly two days, beginning in the Denmark Strait; upon the arrival of *Victorious* Fulmars continued the shadowing, losing two aircraft in the process and her Swordfish made a night torpedo strike, obtaining one hit which had little effect. The *Bismarck* then made for Brest and to anticipate this Force H had moved out from Gibraltar. *Ark Royal*'s Swordfish took up the shadowing after *Bismarck* had been found again by an RAF Catalina. *Ark Royal*'s Swordfish set up a strike but erred and attacked the cruiser *Sheffield* instead. To make amends the Swordfish again struck, this time after dark and this time on the right ship. Two hits were obtained, one of which was vital, damaging the rudders, propellers and steering gear—the ship could now only go in a curving track at reduced speed. The end was now foreseeable as the large ships closed in for the kill, a kill made possible by one air-launched torpedo.

But Force H was principally involved in the Mediterranean and much of this concerned convoy work, principally to Malta, during which there were inevitable air attacks. For many of these trips *Ark Royal* was involved in ferrying aircraft to Malta, principally RAF ones but also some Albacores and Fulmars for FAA operation from Malta. But no ship could survive in such hostile waters for ever and on November 13th *Ark Royal* was torpedoed by U-81 and eventually sank, whilst under tow, almost within sight of Gilbraltar, some of her aircraft escaping to Gibraltar. As a result a squadron of Swordfish and a squadron of Fulmars became shore-based at Gibraltar and attempted to seal up the hole that had admitted the U-boat to the Mediterranean which had destroyed their ship. In this they performed signal service, preventing any U-boat movements through the Straits for about six months.

Not all the Fleet Air Arm's offensive activities were ship-based. We have already seen the activities of 830 Squadron at Malta. During early 1941, with the movements of ships away from the Mediterranean for repair, several fighter squadrons had disembarked at Dekheila, Alexandria and these threw themselves into the fighting with gusto covering convoys in and out of Alexandria and along the coast and generally backing up the RAF in the ground attack work in the desert fighting. For this they used Buffalos, Martlets and Hurricanes scrounged from the RAF. Another disembarked squadron, No 815 with Swordfish, established itself in Crete from where it was well placed to work against the shipping supporting the Italian Greek campaign; it also was based in Greece for a while busily active and was involved in the second pounding given to the Italian fleet, off Cape Matapan in March, 1941. In this 815 joined with *Formidable*'s Albacores and RAF aircraft to slow down the Italian fleet until the Navy's big guns could blow them out of the water. Of four warships only one escaped, the battleship *Vittorio Veneto*.

But what of plans and developments in the Admiralty whilst all these actions were taking place? Although both Matapan and the *Bismarck* affair were great successes they confirmed the old diehards idea that the proper purpose for naval aviation was to slow down enemy vessels for destruction by battleships and cruisers—and this long-held belief in fact hindered the full realisation of the Fleet Air Arm's potential for too long. One of the lessons that had been learnt already was the crying need for fleet fighter aircraft with a realistic performance. The old dictum that carrier-based aircraft would operate outside the range of shore based fighters had proved false in a costly way and was still to prove false. If their Lordships had hoped that the Fulmar would redress the balance they were doomed to disappointment; one event that had stuck in their minds was the ease with which the RAF Hurricanes had flown on and off *Glorious* in the Norwegian campaign without any arresting facilities. The need was urgent and so, when a limited flow of American aircraft became available, one of the most urgently sought classes was that of fleet fighter. Two American aircraft fitted the bill, the Brewster Buffalo and the Grumman Martlet (later renamed Wildcat). These were both ordered and the Martlet became one of the mainstays of the Fleet Air Arm in due course. The Buffalo was an indifferent performer and saw little service. At the same time attempts to navalise the Hurricane resulted in a fighter with a reasonable performance. But first these Hurricanes were to fulfill a more story-book role.

Whilst all that has been recounted of World War II so far has covered the Navy's participation in sea actions and land campaigns by far the most vital function has but barely been mentioned. Britain's greatest vulnerability lay in both wars in her need to bring almost all her vital food and raw materials by sea to the UK. Knowing this the Germans had made use of the U-boat to bring the country almost to her knees in World War I by sinking a sufficiently large tonnage of merchant shipping. That this would again be a main target for German aspirations in any further conflict seems to have gone ill-considered for the provision that had been made to protect the merchantmen was far from adequate. Apart from the immediate attempts at convoy work in the first few weeks of the war, with their disastrous effects, the carrier and its aircraft had been little used to combat the U-boat. Further the Germans were now using long-range aircraft, principally Focke-Wulf Condors, to reconnoitre for convoys and then direct the U-boat packs. This combination had brought the situation to a serious pitch early in 1941 and, as a first step some urgent provision had to be made to deal with it. This first step was very much a random affair intended to deal simply with the Condors. It involved stripping the superstructure off certain merchant ships, and also five RN ships, and installing a catapult, one Hurricane and a pilot. When a Condor approached a convoy the Hurricane would be launched, attack the Condor and then fly to the nearest land or ditch. As can be seen, it was a panic measure and effected very little. The merchant ships' aircraft had RAF crews and the RN ships had FAA pilots; one of the latter, Lt Everett flying from HMS *Maplin* destroyed one FW200 but no other successes were recorded and one pilot was lost.

More effectual was the next step. At last it occurred to the Powers-that-were that there may be a place for a small aircraft-carrier to go along with a convoy to provide eyes and teeth from the air. Accordingly a merchant ship, the *Empire Audacity*, herself a prize captured from the Germans, was fitted up with a small flight-deck. To this came 802 Squadron with six of its Martlet fighters and after a work-up on this miniscule carrier, went to sea on its first convoy duty in September, 1941. This first attempt was more successful than anticipated; not only were enemy aircraft destroyed and driven away but also the Martlets were of offensive value against the U-boats themselves. As the convoys continued so did *Audacity* amass further golden reports. Not only did the Martlets deal effectively with the aircraft but they kept the U-boats heads down and were able to lead the escort vessels to the U-boats. On her fourth and last convoy four U-boats were sunk and two damaged as well as two FW200 Condors being shot down. But the most significant feature was that out of thirty-two ships in the convoy only two were lost. *Audacity* herself was hit and sank but the point had been made. Now the pressure was on to provide more and more of these escort carriers and not only were some ordered from British yards, but from American ones as well. But all this takes time. In the interim the best that could be provided was the CAM Ships with their catapult Hurricanes manned by RAF crews. They soldiered on into 1943, a third of their number being sunk in this period.

The solution to this problem of aerial convoy protection became even more pressing towards the end of 1941 when, with Russia in the war, convoys had to be sent around the inhospitable arctic route to Russia from the UK. To start with the weather on the route was more formidable than anywhere else that convoys were likely to sail; but in addition the convoys had to sail past a considerable stretch of enemy-held coastline (about 1,000 miles) and not many convoys had passed before the Germans saw the opportunity of sealing this source of Russian supply and attacked each convoy with aircraft, U-boats and the surface raiders skulking in the Norwegian fjords. The results were almost catastrophic, culminating in the sinking of 23 out of 36 ships in the fateful convoy PQ17.

The next convoy, which sailed in September, 1942, was accompanied by the escort carrier *Avenger*. Cover of a kind had been given previously; *Argus* had been brought from training duties for the rigours of the Arctic but could only put up two Martlets, *Victorious* had operated in Home Fleet covering operations but this was the first occasion that a specific carrier, fully equipped, had formed part of the convoy. Equipped with three Swordfish and twelve Sea Hurricanes *Avenger* met the large and continuous attacks of torpedo aircraft with bravery; in the first attack they were decoyed and eight ships were sunk. Thereafter the Sea Hurricanes stayed with the ships, time and again breaking up the attacking formations. The three Swordfish were used to spot U-boats and one such was destroyed as a result whilst the Germans admitted the loss of 41 aircraft, two of which were destroyed by a Hurricane from the CAM ship *Empire Morn*. This convoy broke the back of the German's attack and further convoys were subjected to lesser attacks, both in intensity and skill.

At last, it seemed, the Navy had learnt the lesson that convoys needed the presence of a carrier for anti-U-boat and anti-aircraft work—now came the rush to provide sufficient.

Other support had already been given to the Russian campaign when a Home Fleet force attacked Petsamo and Kirkenes in Northern Norway in July 1941. Both *Furious* and *Victorious* were involved in air strikes which did a certain amount of damage, but which were costly in terms of aircraft losses for the defences put up Messerschmitt Bf 109s and Bf 110s which outclassed the Navy's Fulmars. *Victorious* also continued to attack enemy shipping in Norwegian waters, her Albacores mounting up a considerable score as autumn drew into winter. And in the Spring of 1942, whilst providing background cover for an Arctic convoy, *Victorious* met up with the *Tirpitz*, launched a torpedo strike of twelve aircraft. Apparently the strike was a failure, the nearest torpedo being thirty feet away from the ship, but it was to have an important effect for so risky had it seemed to the Germans that Der Führer himself decreed that *Tirpitz* must hitherto not be at sea if there was an aircraft-carrier operating with the Home Fleet. So one unsuccessful torpedo strike virtually bottled up the *Tirpitz* in Norway for the rest of the War.

Whilst these operations were involving the Home Fleet, 1942 had started on a minor key in the Mediterranean. The loss of *Ark Royal* had left Force H without a carrier for the veteran *Argus* was too slow to keep up with the Force. She was ever game, however, and when required would sally forth from Gibraltar with Swordfish and Fulmars to be of such use as she could —her venturings were not very far from home, however. No fewer than four carriers were in re-fit at the time and the newest, *Indomitable*, was assigned to the Far East where War had suddenly sprung a surprise upon the British Empire and forced the US into open conflict. Little carrier activity had taken place east of Suez until early 1941, the only threat being German U-boats and surface raiders but after the destruction of *Admiral Graf Spee* this threat diminished. Carriers had, it is true, played passing games in the Indian Ocean; *Eagle* had been re-fitted in Singapore for service there, only to hasten to the Mediterranean to replace *Glorious*, *Formidable* had attacked Mogadishu on her way to the Mediterranean also, but in February, 1941 the Indian Ocean received its own carrier, the little, old *Hermes* and she promptly set up a blockade of Mogadishu with her twelve Swordfish, being a key factor in preventing Axis shipping from escaping the port. Thereafter she went in search of the surface raider *Admiral Scheer* which was off East Africa but the only contact made was by one of the Fleet Air Arm's catapult aircraft, a Walrus from HMS *Glasgow*. Perhaps fortunately for the Navy this raider moved into the Atlantic on her way back to Germany. The smaller raiders had also met up with these catapult aircraft, both *Cornwall* and *Leander* using Walrus to locate German raiders prior to destroying them.

Hermes herself was used almost continuously on convoy protection duties except for an incursion up the Persian Gulf in April, 1941 when trouble flared up in Iraq. She stayed around there for several months before resuming ocean patrols, eventually going to Simonstown for re-fit in September. The next carrier coming on to this scene was the brand-new *Indomitable*, scheduled to form a vital part of a hunter/killer group in the Far East entitled Force Z with HMS *Repulse* and *Prince of Wales*. This was not to be, however, for she was delayed following a grounding and, before she could reach Singapore, her compatriots had been sunk by air attack on December 10th, 1941, in the war that had broken out with Japan—a further forcible reminder of the penalty of operating ships without air cover.

This advent of Japan forced a new situation east of Suez for here the Navy would, for the first time, oppose a fleet numerically stronger in aircraft carriers. To face this was a new, untried *Indomitable*, and a small, weary *Hermes*; to these two was added *Formidable*. The *Indomitable*'s first task was the melancholy one of ferrying fifty Hurricanes to Java for the remnant of the RAF, fighting a hopeless rearguard action. She then returned to Aden and took a further fifty Hurricanes to Ceylon.

Into this situation, in April, 1942, came a raiding force of Japanese carriers, buoyantly confident after Peal Harbour and Singapore. Fortunately the Eastern Fleet had made their headquarters in the Maldive Islands not, as evidently expected, at Ceylon for it was to Ceylon that the Japanese went. *Hermes* had just arrived there for a short re-fit but otherwise there was little shipping in. The Japanese carrier aircraft made an intense attack on Easter Sunday, destroying more of the RAF's defending Hurricanes than they themselves lost. The same day the Japanese found the two cruisers *Dorsetshire* and *Cornwall* and sank them; meanwhile the Eastern Fleet was searching without success. The Japanese returned to Colombo four days later, to find that the harbour at Trincomalee was empty of shipping, however on the return they sighted *Hermes*, at sea without aircraft, and soon sank her as the shore-based fighters from Ceylon were unable to give her air cover. Then the Japanese force retired to the Pacific for the Battle of Midway and no further Japanese assault force entered the Indian Ocean, a fortunate situation for the Eastern Fleet.

The only further action in this area in 1942 was the occupation of Diego Suarez in May, 1942. For this *Indomitable* left the Eastern Fleet to join *Illustrious* in this attack on Madagascar. Between them they provided copybook air cover, their Albacores paralysing the airfields and their Swordfish bombing and torpedoing French naval units so that there was little or no opposition from ships or aircraft. Thereafter the carrier aircraft spotted for naval guns, maintained air cover and carried out any other jobs that they were asked to do with very little loss to themselves.

But of the three modern carriers in the Indian Ocean at this time only one was to remain—*Illustrious*. Both *Indomitable* and *Formidable* had gone by August, caught up in the troubles of the Mediterranean.

Here the position of Malta was desperate. Already there had been attempts to sustain her and to keep sufficient fighter aircraft there to ward off the enemy air attacks. In these attempts *Eagle* had acquitted herself well, having supplied over a hundred Spitfires in two desperate runs to Malta. Now, in August, one large convoy was assembled (Operation *Pedestal*) with no fewer than four aircraft carriers—*Eagle, Furious, Indomitable, Victorious*. They were to be in company with two battleships, seven cruisers and twenty destroyers, covering fourteen merchant-vessels, all picked because they were speedy enough to keep up with the Navy ships. Sailing through the Gibraltar Straights late on August 9th the convoy remained intact until the first attack by U-boats on 11th during which *Eagle* was torpedoed and sank within eight minutes, a sad loss of a gallant ship. During this time *Furious*, which was acting in a ferry role, was able to fly off her Spitfires for Malta and return to safety. The convoy ploughed on, that evening and the whole of the following day receiving the full brunt of the air attacks; *Victorious* was hit on the flight deck but the fighters from her and *Indomitable* broke up the attacks successfuly until the evening of the 12th when they were saturated by a 100 strong attack. In this attack *Indomitable* received two direct hits and damage below the waterline from a near-miss. Both remaining carriers were now out of action but thirty enemy aircraft had been destroyed for the loss of thirteen. The following day the convoy had to continue without carrier cover with the result that four merchantmen and two cruisers were sunk, but the remnant that reached Malta was enough—enough to save Malta. *Furious* made two more ferry trips that year, flying off Spitfires when within range of Malta and that ensured Malta's survival.

Whilst all this activity had been taking place at sea it was a *sine qua non* that the Air Branch of the Royal Navy had grown considerably at home.

New airfields had appeared and a great training machine had swung into operation with fifty or so second-line squadrons, bases in Ceylon, East Africa and a large training complex at Trinidad in the West Indies. Already the Fleet Air Arm's biggest lack had been met by the provision of Sea Hurricanes and Martlets to ensure an adequate fighter force for the carriers —other new aircraft were being tested, improved and developed. Fleet Air Arm squadrons, as already mentioned, had been involved in action from shorebases, many of the Swordfish and Albacore squadrons operating from UK bases in conjunction with RAF's Coastal Command from time to time. It was one of these which, almost by accident, earned the Fleet Air Arm's third VC.

The battleships and battle-cruisers of the German Navy provided such a potential hazard that British Forces just had to take them seriously and devote much effort to dealing with them, even though they remained in port. Two of these were the *Scharnhorst* and *Gneisenau*, known to the members of HM Forces as the *Salmon and Gluckstein* after the proprietors of a familiar line of teashops. They had had a highly successful frolic in the shipping lanes in 1940 and had retired to Brest where they were joined by *Prinz Eugen* after the *Bismarck* affair. During 1941 these ships took a disproportionate amount of Bomber Command effort in an attempt to destroy them, at their Lordships request, but the bombing was unsuccessful in their destruction and at best kept them in port on the French Atlantic coast. But during the winter of 1941/42 it becoming increasingly apparent to the Allies that these ships would attempt to return to Germany. The attempt was begun on the night of February 11th, 1942 when weather conditions were sufficiently bad to make the attempt possible.

Because the voyage would involve a dash up the English Channel the whole operation largely fell within the province of the Royal Air Force but the Air Branch was in the process of establishing a squadron at Manston 'just in case'. At this time half the squadron, six Swordfish, were in position. The whole operation was an indication of how, with bad weather and unconnected accidents, a complete plan for a particular operation can collapse. Coastal Command was maintaining three different patrol lines to pick up any movement into the Western Channel but due to unserviceability of equipment the passage of the ships coincided with gaps in these patrols. The weather prevented Fighter Command picking them up with their Jim Crow patrol and it was only by sheer chance that two senior officers, on a random hunt for Messerschmitts, flew right over the warships and informed 11 Group that they were found at all. At this stage the forces already laid on for such an eventuality were either moving from one airfield to another or badly placed. Then, when the half squadron of Swordfish, No 825 led by Lt Cdr Esmonde, formed up at Manston only a third of its fighter escort was present. The six Swordfish went in to the attack with great gallantry but to no effect. All were shot down and four men alone were rescued by British MTB's. Further attempts by Coastal and Bomber Command, though bravely made, were ineffectual and the only damage sustained was to the *Scharnhorst* which was slowed down by two mines laid some time previously. Altogether a very sad affair; for his gallantry in leading 825 Squadron Lt Cdr Esmonde was awarded the VC.

1942, for all its heartaches, mistakes and tragic losses can be seen to be the year in which the Fleet Air Arm overcame its major hindrances, evolved the rudiments of its place in warfare and took the ascendancy as the major factor in naval warfare. The need for, and evolution of, a suitable carrier fighter had been met by the Sea Hurricane, the Martlet, and, at last, the Seafire, all of which were operational by the end of 1942. The value of carriers working together both in hunting, convoy escort and supporting military landings had all come to fruition in 1942. The answer to merchant shipping losses had been strikingly demonstrated by the arrival of the escort carriers although their introduction into service was painfully slow. But nowhere was the Air Branch's value more evident than in the Western Mediterranean in November, 1942.

For here was worked out the Allies' most ambitious project yet, the landing of an Army in North Africa to provide one arm of a pincer aimed at driving the Axis forces out of Africa. For this a mighty invasion fleet came together in which US and British forces worked alongside, the naval air contingent comprising five American carriers and seven British carriers. The latter comprised the two fleet carriers *Formidable* and *Victorious*, the two ageing carriers *Furious* and *Argus* and three of the new escort carriers which, it had been hoped elsewhere, would have been providing relief to the hard-pressed Atlantic convoys, losses amongst which were now reaching astronomical figures.

Formidable and *Victorious*, now part of Force H, were primarily responsible to cover the inshore invasion fleets and carriers from anti-submarine attack and the possible interference by Italian-based surface vessels. However, so little was the opposition that their strike aircraft launched into strikes on the enemy's beach-head positions. *Argus* and *Avenger* worked in closely with the landings at Algiers, each carrier having a full complement of fighters for beach-head cover. *Furious, Biter* and *Dasher* did likewise at Oran where they managed to damage or destroy a large number of Vichy-French aircraft ashore. One of the airfields at Algiers, Blida, was captured by a Fleet Air Arm Martlet squadron, No 882, whose CO went into land, covered by the rest of his squadron and took over the airfield until ground forces moved in later in the day. The whole operation was completely and swiftly successful and it was almost entirely due to the fact that the fighter squadrons from the carriers maintained complete air superiority over the landings and their strike squadrons had free run to attack obstinate installations ashore. Only after the whole operation had taken place and the invasion convoys were dispersing did the German Navy appear in force with submarines and nibbled at the convoys; in this way the Navy lost its new escort carrier *Avenger* which, having received one torpedo hit, blew up with less than twenty survivors. Later American carriers were modified by the Navy to prevent such costly losses. By way of recompense *Victorious* and *Formidable* flew some fruitful anti-submarine patrols destroying two U-boats.

Truly, the Air Branch of the Royal Navy had 'arrived' at last; it was now a major factor in the conduct of war at sea and with a mounting number of ships and aircraft coming its way the years ahead were full of promise.

5

Spearhead of the Fleet

'You were wearied with the length of your way but . . . you found new life
for your strength.'   (Isaiah Ch 57)

Although 1943 saw the Fleet Air Arm rise to a position of ascendancy the
observer of the time might have been forgiven if he had not detected this.
The reason for this was the acute shortage of escort carriers, and even those
that did appear were often misemployed on other tasks for which a carrier
was needed. As a consequence convoys were crossing the Atlantic still
generally unescorted by an aircraft carrier and during the first few months
of 1943 the shipping losses rose to a new high total, a figure which, had it
been sustained, would have speedily brought Britain to its knees. *Audacity*
had shown the way but the next few carriers were either diverted to other
tasks or in trouble in one way or another; *Avenger* was lost on Operation
Torch, *Archer* had no end of troubles in herself, *Dasher* blew up in March,
1943 so it was April, 1943 before the next one came into the Atlantic convoy
area. This was *Biter* and on her first convoy one of her Swordfish shared a
U-boat with a destroyer. She thereafter operated regularly across the
Atlantic for over a year. *Archer* joined her and one of her Swordfish used a
new device to sink a submarine; this new device was the air-fired rocket,
carried under the wings of the aircraft for offensive duty against any
likely target. As there was no recoil when fired it could be fitted to any
aircraft and the Swordfish, equipped with them, became a formidable
opponent to surface craft. But *Archer* was still suffering trouble and had to
be laid up before the year was out, having escorted only three convoys.
Tracker came on the scene in September and *Fencer* in October. To those
can be added the MAC ships, merchant ships with superstructure removed
and a flat deck installed converting grain ships and tankers into carriers.
Nine of these entered service as 1943 proceeded and another five in
December and, whilst they never scored any successes against U-boats their
presence was justification in itself for no convoy carrying a MAC-ship
suffered any losses.

One of the big problems that arose at this time was the scale of aircraft accidents. Although the Navy had adopted the American system of having a movable barrier approximately two-thirds of the way up the deck of the carrier far too many aircraft were being lost or damaged through deck accidents. Inevitably any aircraft entering the barrier would, at the best, require a new airscrew. At worst the aircraft could be a write-off and there were occasions when the aircraft floated over the barrier to land with a crunch amongst the aircraft parked forward of it. Other aircraft would veer from the straight and narrow and end up over the side or impaled on the impedimenta to either side of the deck. Seafires were particularly prone to this with their narrow track undercarriage, high ground angle and skittish landing characteristics. It was by no means an ideal carrier aircraft and this problem was never really cured. The extremely high attrition rate was a recurring problem for the rest of the War.

By now, however, new types were entering service. The Martlet, which was already well established in service and did yeoman work through to the end despite being renamed the Wildcat in midstream. 1943 saw the advent of two aircraft from the Fairey stable which had been gestating for overlong. The first, the Barracuda, had been thought of in 1937 and flying in proto-type form since the end of 1940. In appearance it was distinctly odd, the whole thing being built outwards from a central chart room, with bay windows, for the navigator. The wing was just above this and the under-carriage was cranked and folded partly into the wings and partly into the fuselage, except on a heavy landing when the whole apparatus entered the chart room and concertinaed the navigator. The pilot was perched just above the wing at the front of a long greenhouse and the tail was perched near the top of the fin to get it out of the way of the wing's wake. These entered service for torpedo and dive-bombing duties in 1943. The other Fairey product was the Firefly, a fleet fighter of conventional appearance, intended to replace the Fulmar, and it too entered service in 1943 although it was not operational until the following year. Here again it was slower than contemporary fighters, largely because it was a two-seater, and even-tually found its *métier* in the recce and strike role, being successively developed into various marks and finally serving as an ASW aircraft. Blackburns, the other traditional builder of naval aircraft had been working on the Firebrand, but so many problems and changes of mind took place that it was not ready even when the War ended.

Thus the British types for re-equipping the FAA had become a source of frustration and disappointment and the Navy looked to the West for its new hardware. It did not look in vain for the US Navy had been very forward-looking in its procurement. The Fleet Air Arm could pick effective new types straight from the production lines. From the Grumman stable came the Avenger torpedo-bomber and the Hellcat fighter, the latter a replacement for the Wildcat and from Chance Vought the Corsair, a rugged, long-range fighter. These three types, all of which began their British service in 1943, formed the bulk of the Fleet Air Arm's fighting equipment to the end of the War when, as most of them were on lease/lend they were returned to the US or disposed of as required.

With many new squadrons to be equipped with American aircraft the Navy set up a procedure whereby the new squadrons were formed and worked up in the US and then came across the Atlantic to the UK on a carrier, providing convoy protection en route, thus blooding the squadrons and helping the convoy problem at one and the same time.

Inevitably the Royal Navy worked more and more closely with the US Navy. Not only had they common types of aircraft but they aimed, where possible, to standardise practices of operation so that they could be interchangeable. Both services gained by this interchange and 1943 saw the exchange of whole carriers, USS *Ranger* spending a couple of months with the Home Fleet (allowing *Illustrious* to go through to the Mediterranean) and organising a strike against Bodø in Norway on October 4th. They found an unprepared enemy and a full harbour and, for the loss of five aircraft, sank a plenitude of shipping. Earlier, *Victorious* joined the US Navy in the South West Pacific where, as part of Task Group 36.3 from May to July 1943 she provided air cover for the landings on New Georgia. This produced little of interest for her Wildcat fighters, but enabled her Avengers to get some bombing raids in.

In the Mediterranean too there was little for the carriers to do other than convoy escort. With the Axis partners out of Africa the next logical step was Sicily and this could be accomplished with fighter cover from Malta; no carriers were needed. However, one carrier formed part of Force H, *Formidable* and she hovered in the background in case the Italian Fleet should appear. *Indomitable* joined her after nine months repairs and although these two found little action the unfortunate *Indomitable* was attacked by a single Ju-88 which torpedoed her on July 11th and she promptly had to return to dock for another period of just under a year's repairs. Whilst the carriers were not needed for Sicily, the next landing relied entirely on the Fleet Air Arm for its success. This was Operation Avalanche, the cleverly-conceived plan to take the Germans in Italy in the rear and capture a large port into the bargain by landing at Salerno. For this task Force V was formed and on this force the whole operation relied for fighter cover for the landings. Four escort carriers, *Attacker*, *Battler*, *Hunter* and *Stalker* together with *Unicorn* in an operational role at last, equipped entirely with Seafires, one hundred and thirteen of them. Outside this force was Force H, with *Formidable* and *Illustrious* in place of *Indomitable*, once again as an insurance against the Italian Fleet and also to provide protection for Force V itself. As it happened, the Italian Fleet passed nearby as the attack was approaching Salerno but it was on its way to surrender, posing no problems for its old foe, Force H. September 9th was the day of the landings and the Seafires went up at dawn. A continuous cover of twenty Seafires was maintained over the beach-head during daylight hours. The enemy air opposition was light and during the whole operation only two were claimed destroyed and four damaged; by contrast ten Seafires were lost for various hostile reasons. It had been anticipated that the airfield at Salerno (Montecorvino) would have been captured within a day and RAF and USAAF fighters move in but in the event it was not captured for three and a half days and this stretched Force V to its limit for, although only ten Seafires were lost to enemy action more than four times that number were lost due to deck accidents, so temperamental was the Seafire for landing on. *Formidable* and *Illustrious* threw their Seafire components into the force to help but by the time Force V was relieved its aircraft state was pitiable. With the surrender of the Italians and the Salerno landings the Mediterranean Sea became much safer to Allied shipping and both Force H and Force V were disbanded. The escort carriers returned to the UK to re-fit and re-equip, *Formidable* joined the Home Fleet and went to the Arctic extremes for the rest of the year whilst *Illustrious* went through the Suez Canal to join *Battler* as the nucleus of an East of Suez carrier component.

The satisfying pattern of 1943 projected itself into the following year in which the Fleet Air Arm grew by leaps and bounds. More escort carriers brought more operational squadrons from the New World. More training stations in the UK provided more specialised air and ground crew for the carriers. Operational procedures became more and more refined as time went on. At home the convoy battles went on unremittingly; the U-boats would hunt, the convoys would search and occasionally there would be action, at times a ship was sunk, at times a U-boat destroyed, but most of the time the Royal Navy was consolidating its position in a negative way; by keeping aircraft aloft over the convoy the U-boats were kept below the surface and unable to strike. Thus the convoys reached their destinations unscathed, and as month followed month the forces at the disposal of the Home Fleet grew greater and greater. Whilst losses still continued the U-boats were now on the losing side and increasingly they knew it.

As soon as the Spring weather of 1944 gave the Fleet Air Arm clearer skies more offensive activities were planned. There was now only one large surface raider of consequence left in the German Navy (*Scharnhorst* had been sunk by the *Duke of York* at the end of 1943), the *Tirpitz*. If this last thorn in our side could be removed seamen would breathe the easier and forces could be put to other uses. So Operation *Tungsten* was conceived, the target being *Tirpitz* lying in Kaa Fjord, Norway. For this the Fleet Air Arm planned and practised to a high degree. All the 'heavies' of the Home Fleet joined in, the battleships and cruisers providing surface cover for the two fleet carriers *Furious* and *Victorious* which carried the spearhead of the attack, forty-two Barracudas of Nos 8 and 52 TBR Wings. Four escort carriers were called in as well, three of them, *Emperor*, *Pursuer* and *Searcher* providing four squadrons of Wildcats and two of Hellcats to supplement the fleet carriers' fighter squadrons as fighter cover and one, *Fencer* with Swordfish as anti-submarine defence.

The attack, which took the Germans by surprise, went according to the book with Wildcats and Hellcats going in as flak suppression and the Barracudas dive-bombing with great precision. British losses were light and the great vessel was put out of action for another three months with heavy loss of life. Further strikes were made by *Furious* with *Formidable* in July and August but were not so successful as the element of surprise escaped them and the *Tirpitz* was usually covered with a smoke screen. Her final destruction fell to the Lancasters of RAF's Bomber Command, in November. The *Tirpitz* was not the only Norwegian target for the Fleet Air Arm at this time. In these the elderly *Furious* took the lion's share, patrolling up and down the Norwegian coast striking at enemy shipping and minelaying in the Leads. This was her swan song for by the autumn she was much in need of a rest and this grand old carrier, on which the first-ever deck landings had been made, entered honourable retirement in September 1944. Hers had been a tough, relentless war, but one which had finally been crowned with satisfying successes. Others of the fleet carriers operated with her but the brunt of the task was increasingly undertaken by the escort carriers, as were the Russian convoys which continued to provide excitement and hardship. It was now possible to provide two carriers on some of these and the results improved accordingly. Whilst the enemy attacked again and again these convoys now had the measure of the opposition.

1944 was the year of the invasion of Europe, and June was the month of its execution. The mighty thrust across the English Channel, under the code name *Overlord* was encompassed under the overwhelming umbrella of fighters provided by the 2nd Tactical Air Force and the Air Defence of Great Britain. Consequently the role of the Fleet Air Arm was relatively small. However, the Service was there. No 4 Naval Fighter Wing, comprising four squadrons of Seafires, formed a part of the Air Spotting Pool of 2nd TAF and flew tactical reconnaissance sorties during the invasion. No fewer than five squadrons of Swordfish were present for anti-submarine and anti-shipping work generally where their rocket expertise would have been valuable had there been any enemy shipping. These Swordfish were also used to lay smokescreens during the actual invasion. In addition, FAA Wildcats were used to spot for the guns of HMS *Warspite* and other naval ships bombarding the enemy's shore batteries.

However the complementary landings in the South of France in August were another matter altogether as the distance involved meant a strong carrier force to provide cover. From May onwards escort carriers had been arriving in the Mediterranean, some had been working on convoy protection because enemy air attacks had increased once more. All of them had fighter squadrons embarked which had worked-up in the close-support role with the Army. By the time of the landings there were nine carriers, two of them American, with a total of 216 fighters aboard. The invasion began on August 15th and almost immediately the fighters involved were flying in the army support role as air opposition was virtually non-existent. For five days intensive operations were flown with great success and four days later the carriers were able to withdraw as land-based fighter squadrons took over their tasks. Yet another amphibious landing had gone ahead successfully under the umbrella of fleet fighters. The seven British carriers moved across the Mediterranean and during the next two months began a series of successful strikes against the islands in the Aegean, continuing until the main islands had been reoccupied. Thus the Fleet Air Arm's activities in the Mediterranean War drew to a close; two of the carriers returned to the Home Fleet, the others moved through the Suez Canal to join the build-up of forces to prosecute war against the Japanese.

This build-up had grown from the time, in October, 1943 when only *Battler* was providing an air component, with twelve Swordfish and six Seafires. She was joined in January, 1944 by *Illustrious* and they were both based on Trincomalee in Ceylon where a large complex of naval air installations had been built up. Two months later a particular problem in the Indian Ocean was dealt with. German submarines were marauding, kept going by supply ships *Charlotte*, *Schliemann* and *Brake*. They were both despatched by 'R' class destroyers, the second one having been found by *Battler*'s Swordfish.

However, in 1944 the build-up of carriers began. *Illustrious* arrived in January followed by *Unicorn* in her repair ship role. Escort carriers followed, *Ameer*, *Atheling*, *Begum* and *Shah*. In March a Japanese cruiser force ventured into the Indian Ocean from Singapore and sank two ships; *Illustrious*, with escorts, made a sortie to find them, but was unsuccessful, the cruisers retired and the British force returned to what was now a considerable naval base at Ceylon to prepare for offensive activities. These took the form of offensive strikes and were the forerunners of many which would occupy the rest of the War. On April 16th, 1944 a force of twenty-seven ships including *Illustrious* and her American counterpart *Saratoga* set out; the target was Sabang Island, off the tip of Sumatra, an oil port for the Japanese. A considerable element of surprise was achieved and a highly successful strike ensued with the port heavily damaged, the storage tanks destroyed and the nearby airfield strafed involving the destruction of many Japanese aircraft. The only opposition was a torpedo strike as the force was retiring and this was liquidated by the Combat Air Patrol from *Saratoga*.

As a result of this success a further strike was organised, this time on the refinery and port of Surabaya. By contrast, although their losses were light the results were minimal. The same result followed a solo effort by *Illustrious* in June but after this she was joined by *Victorious* and *Indomitable*, the former joining *Illustrious* in a return to Sabang in July; more effective than the last two strikes it did not fully justify the use of these two large ships except insomuch as it was giving the Fleet as a whole and the carriers in particular good training for the future. Further strikes were carried out from time to time together with increased training in weaponry for the carrier squadrons' crews. The next stage in the development of this carrier strike force was to provide a diversionary attack on Car Nicobar whilst the Americans attempted landings at Leyte; this involved the carriers staying in the hostile area for several days. It was carried out with success and provided the first fighter opposition which was taken in its stride by the Hellcat squadrons. The next strikes came at the end of the year at which time *Indefatigable* was added to the force. It now comprised four fleet carriers, the battleship *King George V* and attendant cruisers and destroyers; this potent force entered the New Year as the British Pacific Fleet.

The escort carriers, in the meantime, had been doing what their name implied, although *Ameer* was basically an assault carrier. At the same time as the big'uns moved forward into the British Pacific Fleet so these, together with reinforcements from the Mediterranean, became the East Indies Fleet.

The primary function of this Fleet in 1945 was support of the 14th Army as it swept down through Burma. This was very much the Hellcats' War for in fact the Army called for little in the way of direct support in the ground war. What it did find valuable was the use of the Hellcats in a Photo Recce role, another example of the Fleet Air Arm's flexible versatility, for these aircraft, working often at extreme range, covered 30,000 miles of Malaya for coverage in support of the Army. The Fleet as a whole kept itself busy, at first in support of landings on Ramree Island and Cheduba Island where ground support was needed against the defenders. Further small-scale operations provided useful preparation for Operation *Dracula*, the occupation of Rangoon. For these landings were four carriers, *Emperor*, *Khedive*, *Stalker* and *Hunter*, whilst *Shah* and *Empress* put themselves between this force and Singapore to prevent any Japanese interference from the south. It was all something of an anti-climax as Rangoon was taken unopposed but the carrier crews found many alternative targets in the shape of enemy shipping and airfields. In the event they wreaked considerable damage. They now turned their attention to enemy shipping particularly those attempting to reinforce the Andaman Islands and around Sumatra. The carriers were predominantly flying fighter aircraft at this time and when a Japanese cruiser appeared and required torpedoing the necessary arrangements for launching Avengers with torpedoes became so complicated that in the end she was destroyed by a destroyer flotilla. As the Army swung southwards to the East Indies, the Fleet went ahead striking anything and everything that seemed a likely target, profiting by their past experiences. In what turned out to be their last strikes the Fleet met an attack by *Kamikaze* suicide aircraft, *Ameer* being hit and set on fire but, thanks to the planning put into the ship by the Admiralty, it was not a total loss, returning to base and being ready for action within a fortnight. In the event this next action, the strike on Penang for which six carriers were detailed, never took place for the War was about to end.

In the meantime the British Pacific Fleet had moved on to what was probably the most intensive Fleet Air Arm activity of the whole war. On its way to its new base of Sydney, Australia, the four carriers planned and executed two more strikes, on the two oil refineries at Palembang in Sumatra. These two strikes, on January 24th and 29th, 1945, were carefully planned and turned out to be amongst the most effective carried out by the Navy during the War. One refinery was reduced to one-half capacity for three months and all its storage burnt out, the other was out of action for two months and when it did start again it was at greatly reduced capacity. Arriving at Sydney in February, 1945 the British Pacific Fleet worked hard to ready itself for action with the US Navy and eventually, as Task Force 57, joined Admiral Nimitz on March 26th, charged with sealing the airfields on the Sakashima Gunto whilst the Americans took Okinawa. Four squadrons of Avengers were used to bomb the runways and 'hard' installations, Fireflies from *Indefatigable* (the first squadron of Fireflies to go into action, No 1770) were specifically anti-flak whilst six squadrons of Corsairs and two of Hellcats provided fighter cover over the target and attacked any likely ground targets as a secondary role. *Indefatigable*'s Seafires maintained a Combat Air Patrol over the Task Force as cover for the rest of the strike. All day long the formations went out, attacked, came back, were replenished and re-armed, took off again and so it went on. After two days the Fleet retired to replenish from the Fleet Train, part of which comprised escort carriers, and then back in on March 31st for its next period attacking the same airfields as night after night the runways were repaired and fresh aircraft flown in. In this next phase, at the very time that the landings were taking place on Okinawa, the Japanese took exception to the presence of the BPF and launched attacks with conventional aircraft and Kamikaze. If never before, the decision to make the British fleet carriers heavily armoured paid off now. Whereas a Kamikaze could do serious damage to an American carrier it had only relatively slight effects on the British ones. In this period off the Sakashima Gunto *Indefatigable* took the full force of one on her flight deck at the foot of the island bridge—the carrier was operational again an hour later after the remains had been swept overboard. Five days later *Illustrious* was hit to little effect. Because of their invulnerability the Americans suggested that Task Force 57 would switch their operations and strike against the Kamikaze bases in North Formosa. This they did, from April 11th to 13th and, although hampered by weather, managed to strike again and again at the airfields. The Japanese attempted to retaliate but the fighter cover was most effective and more enemy aircraft suffered than British.

The BPF's absence from Sakashima Gunto had been noted and they were soon requested back; so they returned, *Formidable* having replaced *Illustrious* who was overdue for a re-fit. As before the strikes went in, altogether 50,000lbs of bombs being dropped and then the Task Force and its Fleet Train returned to Leyte for a week's breather after thirty-two days at sea.

The rest over, with plenty of new aircraft and crews, Task Force 57 went back again to the same airfields—to begin with opposition was fierce and more Kamikaze rendered brief pauses, *Indomitable*, *Formidable* and *Victorious* all being hit, *Formidable* twice. The most serious effect was not on the carriers but on any aircraft that happened to be on the flight deck at the time. She also suffered a serious hangar fire which destroyed thirty aircraft but still she fought on with what she had left. The Sakashima raids continued until May 25th when Okinawa had fallen to the Americans and the BPF again retired for rest and replenishment after an intensive two months action. Now the Force returned to Sydney, where it spent June in a full month of resting and repairing. Whilst this was in progress the latest fleet carrier at sea, *Implacable* had arrived to join the Force and set off on her own account, with cruisers and an escort carrier in train to attack Truk. This had been so well worked over by the Americans that there was little left to attack but it served as an excellent final training sortie, bringing the crews up to full operational capability. She rendezvoused with the refreshed BPF at Manus and became an integral part of it. The Force was temporarily reduced to three carriers as both *Indefatigable* and *Indomitable* were still at Sydney repairing, the former rejoining later.

Now designated Task Force 37 the British Fleet had the satisfaction of striking at Japan itself, targets being airfields and rail installations. The force could not work at full strength because of the weather, it being the typhoon season in this area, however the Corsair squadrons managed to make some strikes. The weather also lengthened the RAS (Replenishment at Sea) time and after this the Fleet turned its attention to shipping strikes, one of its bigger victims being the escort carrier *Kaiyo* which was rendered immobile. It is almost incredible that this was the only time the Fleet Air Arm attacked a carrier. Up till this time most operations had been flown by day, however, some of *Indomitable*'s Hellcats of 1844 Sqn had been transferred to *Formidable* and they put up a patrol on the night of July 25th which intercepted a Japanese Navy torpedo attack on the Fleet shooting down three and damaging a fourth—the attack never reached the ships. The routine continued, three days strike followed by two days RAS, except that the RAS periods were extended due to typhoons and, early in August, by the dropping of the first atomic bomb. Operations continued until the morning of the 15th when, almost unbelievably, the War was at an end.

Only a token force of the BPF remained with the US Navy, most of it returning to Sydney where they were met by the 11th Aircraft Carrier Squadron equipped with the newest development in British aircraft carriers, the Light Fleet Carrier. In many ways this was a retrograde step for these vessels were unarmoured, had only short-range defensive guns and a maximum speed of only 25 knots, the idea being that after the War they could be converted to merchant ships. In the event they saw no action, which was probably as well, nor were converted into merchant ships, but provided the backbone of the post-war Fleet Air Arm. The first four of this class, *Colossus*, *Glory*, *Venerable* and *Vengeance* formed the 11th Carrier Squadron and to these fell the task of liberating British territories in Japanese hands.

With hostilities at an end the Fleet Air Arm, in common with all the Armed Forces, was faced with problems. Major amongst these was the question of manpower for the days when all but the youngest and most junior personnel were on long-term engagements were long past, whole squadrons being entirely RNVR-manned. With swift demobilisation the Navy was hampered in its manning problems for some time. But another problem arose, too; most of the FAA's carriers and aircraft had been supplied under Lend/Lease by the United States and under the terms of this Agreement had to be returned or paid for. As a result, the American escort carriers were very soon crossing the Atlantic from whence they had come. This was not too serious a matter for the Navy's commitments were now greatly reduced and could easily be covered by the Fleets and Light Fleets, some of which were still building. The aircraft situation was not so happy for the US Navy had more than enough of its own. So the carriers engaged in the melancholy task of loading up with Corsairs, Avengers, Hellcats and so on, sailing out into deep water and just pushing them over the side. From now on any American aircraft would have to be paid for so the onus once again fell on the British Aviation Industry; what could it provide? From Blackburns, traditional naval aircraft builders, arrived the Firebrand which they had taken the whole war to develop. It entered service within a month of the end of hostilities as the Fleet Air Arm's new torpedo-fighter. Equipping two squadrons at different times, it never really overcame its problems which made it a difficult aircraft for a flight deck with a long-long nose and comparatively narrow track undercarriage. De

Havillands had been developing the Mosquito for carrier operation and the first had landed aboard *Implacable* in 1944, flown by the incomparable 'Winkle' Brown. However, the requirement for a long-range fighter in general and the Sea Mosquito in particular did not really find favour and they served for less than a year. Fairey's had now decided to make capital out of the Firefly and were producing successive variants which became excellent maids-of-all-work, serving the Navy well into the mid-fifties. Supermarines had evolved a replacement for the irreplaceable Walrus, called the Sea Otter, which was an amphibian with a tractor airscrew and more comfortable accommodation but as the Navy was no longer interested in catapults on cruisers only a few were used for communications duties. Shorts produced the Sturgeon to be a carrier-operated long-range recon-naissance bomber with two Merlin engines and a 370mph maximum speed but here again their Lordships waxed indifferent and it suffered the indig-nity of being turned into a target tug. In the event two further piston-engined aircraft arrived to satisfy the Fleet Air Arm's needs in the immedi-ate post-war era. One was the de Havilland Sea Hornet, a single-seat, twin-engined fighter which, converted to a two-seater, radar-equipped affair, became the aircraft on which the Fleet Air Arm really came to grips with night-fighting. The other was the Hawker Sea Fury. This was a simple, logical development from the Tempest F2 of the RAF, it was a rugged, fast, manoeuvrable fighter, amenable to bombs, rockets and other paraphernalia under its wings and was a delight to fly to sea. As partner to the Firefly it became a useful tool into the mid-fifties.

All these developments and re-adjustments took time and in the middle of them the Navy, and it was not alone, was interrupted in June, 1950 by Korea. Almost before she knew where she was the Navy had committed its Eastern Fleet to the United Nations and this Fleet included the Light Fleet Carrier *Triumph*. Aboard was the 13th Carrier Air Group comprising No 800 Squadron flying the ultimate version of the Seafire, the Mk 47, and No 827 Squadron with Firefly FR1's. She began operating off the east coast in company with the US Navy but was soon transferred to the west coast which became, almost traditionally, the British side of things. The Seafires were somewhat of an embarrassment with their long-standing problems but *Triumph* still managed to give a good account of herself until relieved in October by another Light Fleet Carrier *Theseus*. She carried the 17th CAG which had a Sea/Fury Firefly 5 team and was able to enter fully into the scheme of things. But now the Korean weather took a hand, weather that was reminiscent of the Arctic convoys to Russia. However when opportunities arose the *Theseus* was busy flying CAP over the ships, straffing enemy shipping and supporting Army units when strikes were called for. It is quite amazing that in these conditions 1500 sorties were flown in the worst three months and the striking difference between this and the wartime efforts was the complete lack of accidents aboard ship—no longer were the results of a strike to be seen in bent and twisted aircraft on the deck. Then the carrier moved to the east coast where it was more specifically involved in strikes, specialising in bridge-destruction. An American carrier, USS *Bataan*, lent the *Theseus* a helicopter and crew and these were most useful when one or two aircraft did go over the side. By the time she was relieved by *Glory* in April, 1951 she had all but achieved 3500 operational sorties at a higher rate than the American carriers at that time. *Glory* put in five months to be relieved by an Australian carrier with an Australian Air Group, HMAS *Sydney*, also with Fireflies and Sea Furies, then *Glory* returned in January, 1952 for six months after which another Light Fleet, *Ocean* arrived to take up the task. Both *Glory* and *Ocean* encountered the Mig-15 jet fighters which had arrived on the scene but by dint of good airmanship not only did they evade most of these advanced fighters but managed to put paid to the odd one or two, speaking volumes for the Sea Fury and its pilots. So it dragged on, this uncomfortable situation in 'another man's war', to be concluded in July, 1953.

Coincidental with the last throes of Korea was an event of historic significance for the Fleet Air Arm. The new monarch, Her Majesty Queen Elizabeth II, was reviewing her Fleet in the Solent and amongst the serried ranks of ships were no fewer than eight aircraft-carriers including the latest Fleet Carrier, HMS *Eagle*, incorporating much that was the latest in equipment. More significant, perhaps, was the flypast which gave an accurate indication of the changing Fleet Air Arm. Dominating the flypast were the Fireflies and Sea Furies, together with small numbers of other familiar types of piston-engined aircraft. In midnight-blue was a squadron of deep-bellied Douglas Skyraiders, obtained from the United States to provide an airborne early-warning station ahead of the fleet, a new concept we had learnt from the US Navy; also there was another squadron of familiar shapes, Grumman Avengers which 815 were flying as a stop-gap until the new Fairey Gannet came into service. Leading the formation were a few rotating-wings, helicopters which were easing their way gently into Fleet Air Arm service and bringing up the rear were a few, too few, turbine powered Gannets, Attackers, Sea Hawks and Sea Venoms. But they were significant for it is to the helicopters and the jets that we must now turn to see the next big leap forward of the Fleet Air Arm, a leap forward in a way as significant as any in the past. And with it to take the one lingering look back at those Fireflies and Sea Furies; epitomising the great lengths to which the Fleet Air Arm had come during and after the War Years; the Fleet Air Arm was now the Spearhead of the Fleet and the *raison d'être* of much of the Navy's equipment. Almost as a gesture of salute, their Lordships at the Admiralty finally gave ground and re-recognised the name 'Fleet Air Arm' for its naval aviation branch.

6

New Styles, New Heights—New Threats?

'The old has passed away; behold, the new has come.' (2 Corinthians Ch 5)

Korea was full of lessons for the Fleet Air Arm. Whilst it more than endorsed the soundness of the Fleet Air Arm's basic tenets, its training and calibre, it underscored the fact that the Navy had some catching up to do if it was to remain competitive in any further conflict—no more could it be considered reasonable to pit piston-engined Fireflies and Sea Furies against transonic jet fighters such as the Mig-15, no longer was it economic to keep an expensive destroyer or frigate on 'plane guard' duties alongside the carrier whenever flying was taking place when a single helicopter, based on the carrier, could do the job more effectively and more cheaply. And the advent of radical new aircraft would mean that the same style of deck operations just would not do; change must be the order of the day.

It is too easily forgotten that in fact the Navy had led the World initially in its attempts to apply jet aircraft to carrier operation. Scarcely was the War over before plans were afoot to land one of the current jet fighters on a carrier and these came to fruition on December 4th, 1945 when Lt Cdr 'Winkle' Brown successfully landed a 'hooked' Vampire on the Light Fleet Carrier HMS *Ocean*. These were followed up for obviously one landing did not make a fleet jet fighter force. The Meteor was also 'hooked' and tried aboard HMS *Implacable* but its size and configuration hardly made it ideal for the task. It is also interesting to remember that at just this time, 1945-46, one could encounter, in the most unlikely places, a naval officer accompanied by a girder-like contraption, flimsily covered in fabric with a glasshouse at the front and a large propeller mounted horizontally on top. Designated the Hoverfly, this was the first helicopter to go into production, some of which had been bought during the latter stages of the War by the Navy who could see a use for the helicopter as a ship-based submarine spotter. One of these early contraptions actually journeyed aboard a ship on a west to east convoy which was a good start even if it proved very little. But these were beginnings; the Hoverfly could carry very little except for its crew and was so sensitive on the controls as to require one man's full time in getting it safely on and off the ground. The advent of the helicopter in the Fleet Air Arm rested on two things, the development of a practicable helicopter which was easy to control and could carry a load a distance, and the enthusiasm of the Admiralty for the device. In due course the former arrived but in the late forties and early fifties the latter was sometimes hard to detect.

Lack of drive in the Admiralty (or was it lack of purposive direction ?) was hampering matters in the acquisition of jet fighters. Supermarines, who had been good suppliers of naval aircraft down the years, had designed a jet fighter back in 1944, the first prototype flying in July, 1946. Second and third aircraft had been fitted with long-stroke undercarriages, arrester hooks and lift spoilers for carrier operation. One of these began carrier trails aboard *Illustrious* in June, 1947, being successfully concluded four months later. Thereafter ministerial indecision prevailed for two whole years, years in which the US Navy was hampered by no such indecision; at last, in November, 1949 the aircraft, now named the Attacker, was ordered for the Fleet Air Arm. In the meantine a small number of Vampires had been acquired which No 702 Squadron was flying for familiarisation with jet aircraft and means of applying its techniques to naval warfare, and a small number were fitted up for carrier trials. One of the more imaginative of these concerned the carrier HMS *Warrior*. In applying jet aircraft to carriers the idea was mooted that undercarriageless aircraft which were catapulted into the air and recovered by landing on a flexible deck would have many advantages over conventional aircraft. So experiments with Vampires were conducted at Farnborough and then on a rubber deck fitted to *Warrior*. Enough flying was done to prove the concept as practical but the cost of converting the whole of the Fleet Air Arm, and its land aerodromes, to rubber decks and wheelless aircraft just was not on.

In the meantime a combination of inventiveness and plain commonsense on the part of naval officers put the Fleet Air Arm ahead of all comers in the application of faster and heavier aircraft to the aircraft carrier. Problems were rearing their heads in three aspects. The increased weight of military aircraft, and their need for higher take-off speeds, was taxing the limits of the contemporary catapults, working on compressed air and hydraulics. Without increasing ship size, complexity and weight nothing could be done with these catapults but the answer came through the ideas of Cdr C. C. Mitchell who applied steam from the ship's boilers to energise the catapults. Although it took some years to develop this was the perfect answer and has provided the Navy with catapults able to launch any aircraft which could foreseeably come into naval use. Similar limitations were facing the US Navy and they were glad to take advantage of this British invention. They also took up two others which have transformed carrier operation in the jet age. The first of these was brought about largely by the limitations of the human being. The Deck Landing Control Officer, known universally as 'Bats', who had been standing at the side of the deck waving his bats to the incoming pilots to direct their approaches and landings all through the War and after was now coming to the limits of his abilities as the approach speeds of the aircraft went over the 100mph mark; no longer could he easily interpret the position of the aircraft quickly enough to pass it back to the pilot with absolute accuracy in time to enable him to make the necessary control correction. This would be aggravated with the onset of the jet, with its well known lag in throttle response. The answer to this one came from one of the Navy's most eminent glider pilots, Cdr Nick Goodhart, who invented an automatic sight to be installed on the deck roughly where the DLCO had stood. The sight, which was basically a large, curved mirror, had a white light shining on it which the pilot had to keep centred on a line of green datum lights either side of the mirror; this automatically gave him the correct approach as the mirror could be adjusted for the characteristics of each type of aircraft and the sight was also refined to be gyro-stabilised thus compensating for the pitch of the ship. This left the pilot with one problem; how could he keep his eyes glued to the mirror and yet be sure he would not let his airspeed drop too low on the approach? Here science came to his aid by arranging for the airspeed to be relayed audibly into his earphones. These systems have become now the standard method by which the pilot makes his deck-landing approach.

The final limitation to carrier operation which was ingeniously dealt with at this time was one which had, from the very beginning been a problem, but, with the advent of fast landing, heavy aircraft threatened to be catastrophic. This was the problem of coping with the runaway aircraft, the one that missed the wires. As we have seen already, such aircraft arrived at the round-down at or below stalling speed and if it missed the wires either slid over the side or sailed gently into the barrier. Either alternative was expensive and potentially hazardous to life and limb; with the increase in size, cost and complexity of the new generation of jet aircraft this problem was fast becoming prohibitive. It was Captain D. R. F. Campbell, DSC who hit upon the outstandingly simple idea of arranging the landing path of the aircraft at an angle to the fore and aft line of the ship. Whilst this involved building a slight extension to the port side of the ship it meant that the landing path became completely clear of the ship and any aircraft missing the wires could open up and fly around for another landing (such an aircraft soon became known as a 'bolter') without impinging upon any other aircraft on board. This had other advantages in that it allowed the forward part of the deck to be used for other purposes, either as an aircraft park into which landing aircraft would not suddenly be hurled or, and this could be of great operational advantage, allowing other aircraft to be catapulted off forward at the same time as aircraft were landing on. No longer need a carrier be vulnerable to attack whilst landing on. On retrospect it is amazing that no other person had thought of this idea sooner, so simple was it, but its practicability was soon grasped and put into practice as soon as money could allow for the modifications to be put in hand. Typically, the first carrier so modified was an American one, the first British ship thus engineered was HMS *Centaur* which was completed in 1953.

Thus progressed the carrier innovations for the new generation of aircraft; how were they coming along? The helicopter 'arrived' in the Royal Navy with the advent of the Dragonfly, a Sikorsky S51 built under licence in the UK by Westland and powered, in its production version, by a British Alvis Leonides engine. A helicopter squadron was formed at Gosport, No 705, and this carried out pioneer work in developing techniques for operating the helicopter as well as training the generations of helicopter pilots, a task it still carries out at Culdrose in Cornwall. Dragonflies went to sea as plane guards on the carriers and were allocated to Naval Air Stations and it was at one of these, Ford, on the South Coast that Cdr John Sproule invented a scoop net to be used below the helicopter to scoop ditched airmen out of the sea. The Navy's helicopters came into prominence in early 1953 when 705 Sqn decamped to Holland and carried out sterling work in the disastrous flood areas there. By that time, however, the first practical load-carrying helicopter, the Whirlwind, was beginning to enter Naval service. With this machine the Navy turned from using the helicopter as an adjunct to naval flying into using it as an airborne weapon system.

By this time the Navy's first jets were in operation. No 800 Squadron had received its first Attackers in August, 1951 at Ford and just over a year later took them afloat in HMS *Eagle*. As a jet fighter the Attacker was no star performer and its tailwheel undercarriage made it less than efficient on carrier decks but it served its purpose in giving the Fleet a jet fighter to work up as an operational element and upon which tactical methods could be worked prior to the arrival in service of the Seahawk.

Steadily the metamorphosis of the Fleet Air Arm from piston-engined fixed-wing aircraft to jets and helicopters continued. In 1952 the first Whirlwinds arrived, imported ones from America as Westlands had not yet established a production run. These Whirlwinds were formed into a squadron at Gosport for a very different role, being transported to Malaya where the British land and air forces were engaged in a bitter and frustrating fight against the Communist terrorists. Here they lost all pretence of naval operations and threw themselves into the jungle warfare, carrying soldiers from place to place around the jungle, landing in tiny clearings, rushing the wounded to hospital and perhaps more significantly, opening the eyes of the British military to the revolutionary practicabilities of the helicopter in land warfare. This Squadron, No 848, literally pioneered what has now become the commonplace activities of the RAF and Army helicopters as well as triggering off the thinking in the Navy which has led to the Commando carriers of which more anon. For four years this squadron with twelve helicopters, soldiered on providing a unique service and assisting in no small measure to defeat the terrorists. On its return to the UK it was to a Fleet Air Arm which had blossomed into the new jet age and in which the helicopter was about to take on an important new role.

In the meantime the Admiralty had gone ahead with planning a new turbine equipped force. The interceptor and strike fighter was to be the Hawker Seahawk, the all-weather fighter, following on the work of the night-fighter Hornets, was to be the de Havilland Sea Venom, a twin-boomed fighter evolved from the Vampire. For torpedo and rocket strike was coming along the Westland Wyvern, a large, single-seat turboprop machine, Westland's last fixed-wing production and for anti-submarine work was the Fairey Gannet, similarly powered by turboprops and with a capacious weapons bay for expunging submarines. These types all entered service during 1953 and 1954, having had varied developmental careers, and for them came the additional carriers, *Centaur*, *Albion* and *Bulwark* and the new fleet carrier *Ark Royal*, bearer once more of that famous name. Never, since the outbreak of peace, had the Fleet Air Arm's importance and ability to fulfill its role seemed more sure and certain.

It was not long before this country received quick confirmation of the perennial need of a carrier force to a nation such as ours which is dependent on sea routes and overseas contacts but yet cannot rely on safe overseas bases.

When it became politic to the British and French Governments, to secure the Suez Canal in November, 1956 because of the Israeli/Egyptian situation, Operation Musketeer was put into execution. This involved the taking of the Canal Zone and the neutralisation of opposing (Egyptian) forces. Great Britain was immediately put in something of a quandary because its two sovereign bases, Malta and Cyprus, were too far away from the seat of action to enable adequate fighter cover for such operations and in fact the two squadrons of Hunters sent to Cyprus were little used for this reason. That such a condition would be normal and become even more frequent as the British Empire continued to disintegrate had not been lost on the Navy; it was therefore to the Fleet Air Arm that the British Government looked for the close air support necessary and did not look in vain for, mustered in the Mediterranean, was a force of five carriers. The one Fleet carrier, HMS *Eagle*, carried one squadron of strike Wyverns, two of Sea Venom fighters and two of Seahawks together with an early warning flight of Skyraiders. *Albion* had another flight of Skyraiders and a force of two Seahawk squadrons and one Sea Venom squadron and *Bulwark* three squadrons of Seahawks. *Ocean* was operating in the tentative role of a Commando carrier with one squadron of Whirlwinds whilst *Theseus* had embarked the Joint Experimental Helicopter Unit with its RAF Whirlwinds and Sycamores. Two French carriers were also in attendance equipped with Corsairs and Avengers, an interesting comparison of wartime aircraft with the new generation Fleet Air Arm.

After the first attacks made on the night of October 30th by RAF Canberras the carrier aircraft provided air cover over the Zone by day and, more particularly, provided a recurrent strike force against all the Egyptian airfields, concentrating on those in the Delta area. This was maintained for the next four days and when the paratroop force flew in on November 5th the fleet fighters gave continuous air cover. This was followed up the following day by the Navy's own airborne landing when *Theseus* and *Ocean* used their helicopters to land 45 Royal Marine Commando and to follow up with a casualty evacuation service to the carriers lying offshore all operating under the Fleet's air umbrella. That night the ceasefire was called after which it was mainly the task of the helicopters to clear away the remnants.

When the final count was over the Fleet Air Arm's operations had been carried through at the cost of two Seahawks and two Wyverns. The work of the carriers had been highly successful, confirming the dictates of the years since the War, reflecting lessons learnt from the War and underscoring the vital need to this nation of just such a force of flexible airfields as a carrier force provides. The activities of *Theseus* and *Ocean* were so promising as to give the go-ahead for the concept of the Commando Carrier and its Marine Commando Force. The emphasis put on the Fleet Air Arm as the premier force of the Navy could be seen to be right; but, and it was a big but, because of the political overtones and the unexpected disapproval of Britain's biggest ally the name 'Suez' became as a stench in the world's nostrils and its effect more far-reaching on Great Britain than any reverse before or since. For Suez marks the moment since which Britain's voice has faltered in the world and Britain's politicians have failed to regain that confidence which has always been the hallmark of British policy since the days of the first Elizabeth. Though the Fleet Air Arm's part was brilliant, the effects of Suez have, in a measure, been a contributory factor in the troubles that have plagued the Naval Air Arm in the 'sixties and 'seventies.

One age-old legacy of carrier operation the Fleet Air Arm had not yet overcome: the widely-held belief that of necessity the carrier-borne aircraft had to be inferior to its land-based counterpart. Of the four standard types flying at Suez only the Seahawk was an outstanding aircraft and this was no match for the Hunters, Super Mysteres, Thunderstreaks and Mig-17's which were its equivalents in the world's Air Forces. But within the next few years this age-old belief was at last refuted and the Fleet Air Arm received aircraft for which it had to apologise to no one. Ever since the Attacker of the early 'fifties Supermarines had been steadily developing the naval strike fighter, sweeping the wings, putting on tricycle undercarriage, then blowing up the design to carry two engines, at first with a butterfly tail and then with a conventional one—a whole string of prototypes which appeared at successive SBAC Displays, were embraced by the Aeroplane and Armament Experimental Establishment at Boscombe Down, and then disappeared, subsequently appearing in a technical training school or on a scrap dump years later. But in 1956 the latest in this line formed the subject of a production contract and there emerged a most advanced strike fighter with what many consider to be the most beautiful lines of any naval aircraft. It was named the Scimitar and the first operational squadron formed at Lossiemouth in 1958, going aboard HMS *Victorious* subsequently. This was the same *Victorious* of war days, being the only wartime fleet carrier still in existence and remaining in service, with massive refits, until 1967. The Scimitar in due course replaced the Sea Hawk although the latter was a long time a-dying and remains one of the memorable post-war Fleet Air Arm types. Likewise a successor for the Sea Venom was soon to follow; in fact it had been flying in prototype form since 1951 as the DH 110, one of the first British aircraft to exceed the speed of sound. Its development was blighted by the accident to the prototype at Farnborough in 1952 in which John Derry and his observer were killed but after the second prototype had been partially navalised and flown on and off *Albion* another prototype was further navalised, carrying out extensive carrier trials on *Ark Royal* in 1956. Such was the promise of this type that it was ordered into production and the first squadron of Sea Vixens (as the type was known) was formed in 1959. At last the Fleet had an all-weather, air superiority fighter that was more than a match for most other fighters, certainly it compared favourably with the Javelin, the RAF's equivalent and as time went on it was to prove a potent strike aircraft also, with a variety of bombs, long-range tanks and rockets on its six underwing pylons. It was the Sea Vixen that brought the Fleet Air Arm into the missile age, being equipped with Firestreak air-to-air missiles.

At about this time the Gannet's replacement entered service, although the Gannet was far from outmoded. But the decision had been made to make anti-submarine warfare the primary province of the helicopter and Whirlwinds, equipped to carry torpedoes and mines, and fitted with the new dipping sonar, began to enter service in 1958. Their advantage was that they could go into the hover, lower the sonar into the water and listen out in a specific spot. By placing a formation of helicopters in suitable positions a far-reaching sonar cover could be obtained. There was subsequently a hiccough in this programme when it was found that too many Whirlwinds were making unpremeditated descents into the 'oggin (as the sea will always be known to the Navy) and the Gannet had to be re-introduced but this was only a temporary phase and was eventually remedied.

But already there were straws in the political wind which, before long, were to spell alarm to the Fleet Air Arm. In 1957 there emerged the Sandys White Paper on Defence which, at the time, hit hardest at the Royal Air Force for its tenet was that the manned aircraft was finished, all was to be missiles. Promising aircraft projects, principally for the Air Force, were stopped overnight but the Navy was told that it would be reduced in size, that the submarine, missile-equipped, would be the capital ship of the future and that the RNVR Air Branch was to be disbanded.

This latter had been created in 1946 out of a nucleus of wartime Fleet Air Arm members who wished to continue as a reserve and who flew at week-ends and in their spare time. Evolving in a similar pattern to the Auxiliary Air Force squadrons it had units based at Abbotsinch for the Scots, Stretton for Northern England, Bramcote for the Midlands, Culham, then Benson for the London area and Ford for the South. They were equipped with current naval types and provided an enthusiastic reserve of a very high quality. They graduated to jets with Gannets, Attackers and Seahawks only to be brutally chopped by Sandys at the same time as the Royal Auxiliary Air Force squadrons in 1957. The carrier force was reduced at about this time, *Unicorn*, the depot carrier, and the Korean trio *Glory*, *Ocean* and *Theseus* together with *Bulwark* were withdrawn, the latter for rebuilding as a Commando carrier.

It was in this new role that *Bulwark* takes the centre of the scene in the next emergency which came the Navy's way. In 1961 the tiny sheikdom of Kuwait in the Persian Gulf found itself at the receiving end of thunderings from Iraq, next door. Fearing for its independent existence it appealed for protection from Britain. Within a day *Bulwark*, who was 'down the road' at Karachi had arrived on the scene before any other British forces. She put 42 Marine Commando ashore by means of her Whirlwind squadron (No 848). These held the situation until RAF and Army forces moved up from Aden. In the meantime *Victorious*, at Hong Kong, had sailed and arrived at Bahrein in ten days. With her new radar equipment she was able to set up a mobile air defence control centre which served the RAF as well as the Fleet Air Arm units. Her early warning aircraft, now modified Gannets in place of the American Skyraiders, were instrumental in giving long-distance radar cover for the British forces. Yet again the crisis which, fortunately, did not involve a hot war, proved how vital a viable carrier force was to a national whose vital supplies come from far overseas.

In the same year as Kuwait the helicopter side of the Fleet Air Arm received a filip with the entry into service of the Westland Wessex. This, like its predecessors, was a licence-built Sikorsky designed helicopter re-engined with, in this case a British jet engine, the Napier Gazelle. Whilst the Whirlwind had been working almost at its limits, especially in hot climes, the Wessex had plenty in hand and this new helicopter enabled the Fleet Air Arm to exploit the helicopter's ability much more fully; it entered the anti-submarine role in 1961 and the commando role a year later. The other new aircraft that entered the Navy at that time had been developed as the NA 39 by Blackburn's, for some years without its customary naval aircraft in service, and proved to be such an advanced and important aircraft, especially in its re-engined Mark 2 version, that, nine years later, it entered service with the Royal Air Force as its principal strike aircraft. This, the Buccaneer, was designed for low-level, long-range bombing and was specially designed to be rock-steady flying at just sub-sonic speeds near the ground. Able to deliver nuclear stores if necessary, it gave the Fleet Air Arm a capability second only to the US Navy in terms of seaborne aircraft. Somehow it seemed fitting that after preliminary trials aboard *Ark Royal* the first squadron of Buccaneers should be based in *Victorious*, that grand old lady still earning her keep through the 'sixties. Add to this the fact that the new super carrier CVA-01 was in the planning stage and the Fleet Air Arm had come to stay, its role being clearly acknowledged as vital to the nation's future, at least for the foreseeable future.

It was no surprise, to the Fleet Air Arm at any rate, that when the next spot of bother in which Britain was involved happened at the end of 1962 a carrier was soon there to add practical weight to Britain's word. As the new Federation of Malaysia was born Indonesia saw this as an opportunity to bite a bit off before it could say no and took a nibble at North Borneo at the end of 1962. *Albion,* now converted as the second Commando carrier, was in the Indian Ocean with the first squadron of Commando Wessexes and another of Whirlwinds; she made for North Borneo and these two squadrons (845 and 846) put 40 Marine Commando ashore and then proceeded to go into the forward line to support the troops there. It was all very similar to 848's activities in Malaya ten years before except that back at the coast was *Albion* who was later relieved by *Bulwark* providing support. Like 848, the work went on for years, the last helicopter not leaving until October, 1966 during which time the squadrons had done a prodigious amount of work known only to those on the spot. Once again a carrier on the spot had provided timely assistance.

Whilst this was going on the original dreams of those aviators who, during the War had put one of Sikorsky's early helicopters on a ship for a convoy patrol came to fruition. After a long gestation period the Westland Wasp helicopter evolved from the original Saunders-Roe P 531. Much experimental work had been carried out on small platforms on frigates and the problems ironed out so that when 829 Squadron was reformed in 1964 and based at Portland it was as a headquarters unit supplying small flights to frigates of the Navy for anti-submarine detection and destruction. Thus the development of the helicopter in the Navy had gone full circle to its originally intended role. The Wasp, as it worked out, made an ideal helicopter for the task and those who serve in the small flights have the peculiar satisfaction deriving from a small team of men doing a challenging job 'at the sharp end'. Equipped with depth charges or torpedoes and now with missiles the Wasps provide a far-ranging protection against submarines. In due course this developed into placing Wessexes on similar platforms on the 'County' class destroyers and certain Royal Fleet Auxiliaries. Looking further ahead was the comforting thought of one hundred and thirty-eight McDonnell F-4K Phantom supersonic fighters ordered, for use on CVA-01 and on the present fleet carriers suitably modified.

It was also in 1964 that an historic change affecting all the British Services took place for in that year the Ministry of Defence was formed, taking under its umbrella the Admiralty, War Office and Air Ministry which all ceased to exist. That the Royal Navy should no longer look to the Admiralty after centuries of so doing but had to deal with the MOD (Navy) must have made people like Pepys, Nelson, Beatty and others revolve in their graves, poor souls. The Fleet Air Arm took it phlegmatically, what else could it do, but felt, perhaps, that it boded ill; just how ill they were to find out as the years unfolded.

The next spot of bother affecting British overseas interests arose out of the Rhodesian UDI row and the subsequent oil embargo. To carry this out *Eagle* was sent to the Mozambique Channel where its aircraft wore themselves out patrolling for any likely blockade runners. This began in March, 1966 and has been carried out since *Ark Royal* relieved *Eagle* and followed the same pattern of somewhat wasteful flying. But in 1966 the Fleet Air Arm received the first of a series of shocks when Denis Healey's Defence White Paper cancelled the new carrier CVA-01 outright and gave no viable alternative. Although those in Whitehall might not have been surprised it caught the Fleet Air Arm at the Air Stations and afloat on the raw, they could hardly believe it. Slowly during the next few years it dawned on them that the very existence of the Fleet Air Arm as they knew it was at stake and the fight began—echoes of the old battles against Trenchard in the early 'twenties maybe but now the enemy was not, primarily, the Royal Air Force, although their ideas for alternatives to the Fleet Air Arm did not prove exactly helpful, but the bureaucratic overlords who, as the Navy saw it, were more concerned with padding the buttresses of the welfare state than preserving the sea routes which were the life blood of the nation. So the Fleet Air Arm, off its own bat, took every opportunity of displaying its vigour and efficiency to the British nation, a typical example being the 1966 SBAC Display at Farnborough which was one of unusual dreariness enlivened well and truly by *Hermes* Carrier Air Group which, ashore at the time, provided a most realistic and breathtaking attack on the airfield.

The paradoxical situation had arrived that the Fleet Air Arm had reached its peak pitch of efficiency at last with aircraft in service and about to enter which would maintain it in the front rank for many years, and yet the Defence Statement of 1967 could make such comments, almost in the same breath, as 'Air power will be as indispensable to the Fleet of tomorrow as it is today'. 'After the last carriers go the Royal Navy will rely on Royal Air Force land-based aircraft to support it.' Remarks such as these, made at a time when RAF bases around the world were dwindling each successive year and those few remaining were becoming more and more politically compromised, might have sounded fine to the taxpayer; to the Navy they sounded not simply comical but grave indeed.

The Phantom arrived on the scene in 1968, not the 138 originally ordered for the Navy but a mere twenty-eight, just sufficient to maintain one squadron aboard *Ark Royal,* the one carrier which was being modernised to last into the early 'seventies. The Fleet Air Arm refused to be daunted and continued to fight on providing as ever a highly efficient performance both at Air Stations and aboard ships. It was at this time that the 'Fly Navy' campaign broke out, almost spontaneously within the ranks and the expression appeared in the most unexpected places, followed by an outbreak of variant slogans, evidence of the determined belief by the men of the Fleet Air Arm in the rightness and value of the job they were doing.

As well as the mighty Phantom another new helicopter joined the FAA at this time. From the Westland stable came the Sea King, again a modified version of the Sikorsky Sea King incorporating British radar and anti-submarine equipment, lifting the ASW capability of the squadrons way up in terms of endurance and range. By 1970 the Fleet Air Arm had been reduced to two fleet carriers: *Eagle* and *Ark Royal* and two commando carriers, with one of the retired fleets about to be converted to replace a commando carrier. Also in service was *Blake,* a converted *Tiger* class cruiser which had become a helicopter carrier, a strange beast reminiscent of some of the World War I attempts at planning an aircraft carrier, having a flying off platform aft, behind the superstructure and capable of carrying a scaled down squadron of Wessexes or Sea Kings and thus providing something of an anti-submarine force.

Once the writing on the wall was plain for the Fleet Air Arm to see the fixed-wing brigade were given options of leaving, joining the RAF or transferring to helicopters or other branches of the Navy. Typically, many of them hung on to see whether a change of government in 1970 would reverse the fate but when this only brought an elongation of *Ark Royal*'s existence and no future fixed-wing programme for the Navy there was little left to stay for, the run-down had passed the point of no return.

Despite this the Fleet Air Arm, as this is written, is still a potent force. *Eagle* with her Sea Vixens, Buccaneers, Sea Kings and early-warning

Gannets lives on for a while and *Ark Royal*, the pride of the Fleet Air Arm, carrying a similar complement but with Phantoms instead of the Vixens, will soldier on formidably for some years. The helicopters of the Navy are fulfilling many roles quite indispensably and their future is bright as long as the Navy has ships and a job to do. What the future holds no one can say at this juncture for rumour follows rumour and talks of V/STOL carriers are bandied about almost carelessly. Incredibly as it may seem, this nation which twice this century has been almost brought to its knees by submarine warfare, when faced at the present with a rapidly expanding and increasingly daring Soviet Navy, can almost scuttle the most effective means of dealing with such a menace, the aircraft carrier force, and then dither, not knowing how to fill the gap. Whatever transpires, sufficient has been seen of the Fleet Air Arm down the years for the Fleet Air Arm of the present day to perpetuate its name in terms of glorious service and supreme skill.

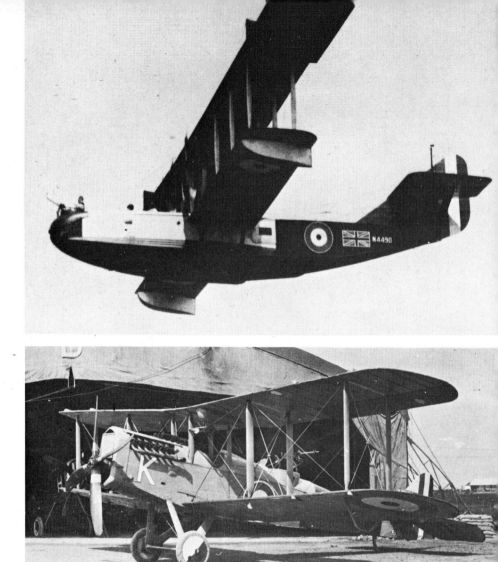

Top: Following on from the *Large America* came John Porte's successful Felixstowe F.2a. This took the Curtiss boat's general layout but remedied its weaknesses and was the mainstay of the anti-submarine forces for the rest of the war. This particular aircraft, N4490 *Aquila*, went on to serve with No 267 Squadron, RAF, in the Mediterranean. [MOD

Above: Following on from Cdr Samson's original bellicose activities, the RNAS always had a penchant for taking the battle to the enemy. Therefore, on amalgamation with the RFC into the RAF, it provided a sizeable day bomber force equipped, for the most part, with Airco D.H.4s. No 202 Squadron (ex 2 Squadron RNAS) was at Berques in July 1918 and 'B' Flight's hangar is shown with D.H.4 N5968 standing outside.[N. FRANKLIN

Right: All around the UK coast the RNAS built up costal patrol stations equipped with landplanes, seaplanes or flying-boats. This one, believed to be Cattewater in Plymouth Sound, stowed its short 184 seaplanes along the mole with a steam-driven crane on a railway which moved along to lower individual aircraft into the water.

[VIA R. C. JONES

Top/Above: Brainchild of Admiral Sir Murray Sueter and Sir Frederick Handley Page, the big Handley Page 0/100 night bombers formed the most effective piece of offensive equipment in Allied use when the RAF was formed. These scenes show one of No 214 Squadron's aircraft outside the hangars at Condekirke in June 1918 . . . . . . and the refuelling operations necessary to tank one up for the night's raid. [IWM

Right: In July, 1918 HMS *Furious* set out into the North Sea, her fore-deck carrying a small force of Sopwith 2F1 Camels with bomb-racks and upper-wing roundels obscured. In due course they took off and set off to the mouth of the Elbe where, at Tondern, they bombed the airship sheds, destroying Zeppelins L54 and L60. One Camel was lost, three landed in Denmark and the other three ditched, alongside *Furious*. [IWM

Below: The classic aircraft carrier at last appeared in October, 1918—too late for action. She was HMS *Argus* and was completed with a completely flush-deck, the exhausts being discharged at the stern. Below her flying-deck was one long hangar with lifts fore-and-aft. This photograph shows the hangar looking aft. In the foreground are two Sopwith Camels, one about to be winched on to the rear lift. Beside the rear lift, with its wings folded, is a Sopwith Cuckoo, the Fleet's first torpedo-bomber designed as such. Aft of the lift are stowed Short 184 seaplanes. [IWM

Above: With the end of the War the lighter-than-air side of Naval flying had reached the stage of acquiring rigid airships such as HMA R23, shown here with the large ground-handling crew required. This airship entered service in September 1917, being powered with four Rolls-Royce engines of 250hp each and having fore and aft control gondolas. It was based at Howden. [IWM
Left: The R23 was used in experiments with carrying its own fighter aircraft and releasing them in the air. Lt R. E. Keys DFC of No 212 Squadron RAF is flying this Sopwith Camel immediately after release from R23. [IWM

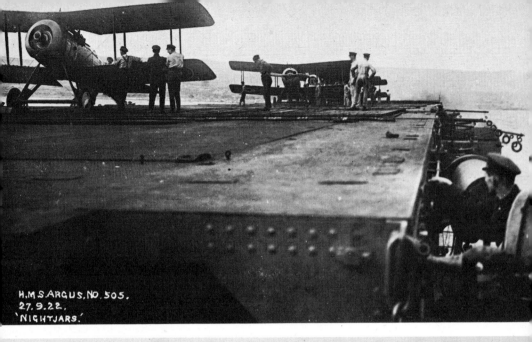

H.M.S.ARGUS,NO.505,
27.9.22,
'NIGHTJARS.'

Top: The first Fleet fighters to serve on the new HMS *Argus* were Nieuport Nightjars, similar, except for power plant, to the RAF's Nighthawks. Six of them served with No 401 Flight afloat in 1922 and 1923 and also with No 203 Squadron during the Turkish crisis of 1922. 203 Squadron was transported to Turkey aboard HMS *Argus*.

Above: Ugliness epitomised the naval aircraft of the early twenties and the Westland Walrus was no exception. Forced to use surplus DH9 wings, the aircraft was characterised by odd bumps and bulges to cope with the varied operation of tasks envisaged for it. The scaffolding in front of the undercarriage was to comply with early attempts at arresting the aircraft on landing, the "clothes pegs" on the axle being to engage horizontal wires along the carrier's deck and the skid to stop the aircraft nosing over.

Above: Many devices were tried to overcome the problems of landing on aircraft carriers. One of the most persistent ideas was a trap of longitudinal wires which kept the aircraft straight (in theory) and on which hooks on the axle engaged to decelerate. A Sopwith Camel is shown in such an arrangement; the small tip clearance between the airscrew and the wires was not a good idea. [MOD

Below: This photograph gives a good idea of the advance which *Argus* gave in landing capabilities. The stern exhaust can be seen below the deck, the handling crew are standing each side of the deck ready to grab the Blackburn Blackburn as soon as it was settled. [HEARN VIA R. C. JONES

Above: The Blackburn Blackburn was one of those unlovely naval aircraft of the twenties. Built around the requirements of the observer who had a palatial cabin with four portholes, the pilot was stuck way up just below the leading edge of the top wing and there was a gunner's position aft (into which a mechanic is just climbing). These aircraft are believed to belong to 422 Flight which served on both *Argus* and *Eagle*.

Below: Contemporary with the Blackburn was the Avro Bison. Its configuration was similar giving such a built-in headwind that its 450hp Napier Lion II engine was doing well if it could raise its maximum speed to the official 110mph. This particular aircraft is shown carrying out a task to which most naval aircraft were allotted towards the end of their careers; that of towing a target for fleet gunnery practise.

Top/Above: The Fairey Flycatcher was one of the Navy's classic aircraft. A fleet fighter par excellence it was also a joy to fly and to behold flying. It could be used as a landplane (this aircraft is from 403 Flight, HMS *Hermes*) . . .

[REAL PHOTOGRAPHS

. . . or as a floatplane, for operation from the catapults of battleships or even the decks of aircraft carriers on trolleys.
[F. E. LUCOCK VIA M. GARBETT

Above: Towards the end of the War the Fairey Company had developed a series of floatplanes, none of which entered service at that time. The line was delevoped and went into service with the Fleet Air Arm as the Fairey IIID in 1924 both as a floatplane and a landplane. It was Fairey IIIDs of No 441 Flight aboard HMS *Argus* which were used in the first of the Fleet Air Arm's *fire-brigade* operations. This took place at Shanghai in 1926 when the Flight went ashore to Shanghai racecourse to defend British interests during the fighting. The crew in front of this IIID on the racecourse are Lts Price and Bayliss with RAF groundcrew. [VIA R. C. JONES

Below: The torpedo-bomber role was adequately fulfilled when the Blackburn Dart came into Fleet Air Arm service and it was with this type that this form of warfare was made practical. This particular aircraft has been painted overall in RAF night-bomber green (known as 'Nivo') for night operations, carried out afloat in the early thirities. [MOD

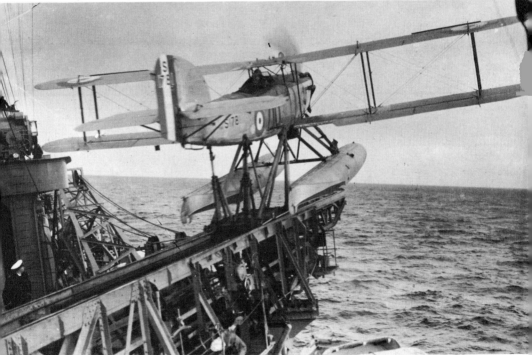

Top/Above: The Fairey IIIF was the outstanding general-purpose aircraft of the Fleet between the Wars. It served in Torpedo-Spotter-Reconnaissance squadrons such as this 823 Squadron aircraft flying from HMS *Glorious*. . .

. . . and as a floatplane in the Catapult Flights aboard battleships and cruisers. S1781 is here leaving HMS *Exeter*: note the four attachment points on the fuselage and the hook above the wing for recovery.
[FLIGHT

Above: Symbol of the new-style
aircraft-carrier was HMS *Courageous* which
appeared on the scene in 1928. She had her
funnel on the starboard side (as *Eagle* and
Hermes) with a bridge built on foward,
hangar doors at the front of the flight deck
and a slip deck forward of that. Flycatchers
would fly out of the hangar and off over the
bows. [REAL PHOTOGRAPHS

Right: Aerial view of HMS *Eagle* in the early
thirties gives a relatively good idea of the
proportions of *Eagle* for touchdowns and
take-offs. The aircraft to take-off are ranged
aft but forward of the round-down. In this
case they are two Fairey IIIFs, and four
Blackburn Ripons. The ship steams into wind
as shown by the smoke-streamer on the
bows. Most of the deck-handling crew stand
about the island, two men crouch on the deck
holding chocks to the aircraft taking off. The
first Ripon '64' is two-thirds of the way down
the deck keeping to the painted centre-line,
the next one begins to taxi out to the chock
men. Each aircraft has a handler at each
wing tip.

Top/Above: The early 'thirties saw a spate of new biplanes entering Fleet Air Arm service. Many of these were developments of existing machines. In the torpedo-bombing field the Dart was refined into the Blackburn Ripon in 1929 seen here dropping a 'tin-fish' . . .

. . . and here in one of those poignant carrier moments. What was about to happen? In the event the aircraft fell over on to the slip deck of HMS *Glorious* just below the flight deck.

Above: The Ripon then was re-engined and became the Blackburn Baffin. *Courageous's* 810 Squadron are seen taking off from one of the Fleet Air Arm's peacetime shore stations, Gosport. [THE AEROPLANE

Below: One of the developments which did not get very far and had tragic results was the building of the submarine M2 which contained a hangar forward of the conning tower and catapult ramps ahead of this. Parnall's built the two-seat Peto for operation from this hangar. The whole enterprise collapsed when the M2 was lost off Weymouth, possibly due to the opening of the hangar. [FLIGHT

Above: The Fairey IIIF was developed into the Fairey Seal with an Armstrong-Siddeley Panther IIA engine and new fin and rudder. These Seals in tight formation over Kowloon Harbour, Hong Kong, belong to 'B' Flight 824 Squadron. [VIA CHAZ BOWYER

Below: The biggest step forward in the new biplanes from the performance point of view was the Hawker pair of fighters, the single-seat Nimrod and the two-seat Osprey. The Nimrod, this one is from 800 Squadron on HMS *Courageous*, was developed from the Hawker Fury. [VIA R. C. JONES

Top/Above: The Osprey operated in two roles, as floatplane for catapulting from cruisers, this one being from HMS *Norfolk* . . . [G. B. HOLLAND VIA B. J. LOWE

. . . and as part of the complement of the Fleet fighters squadrons on the carriers. An 800 Squadron Osprey taxies up the deck of HMS *Courageous*. [FLIGHT

Top: HMS *Courageous* was the carrier upon which the final form of aircraft arresting was evolved. Transverse wires were stretched across the rear end of the flight deck and these were engaged by a hook suspended from the aircraft. After refinement this became the standard means of arresting aircraft thereafter. The new generation of aircraft were designed with hooks from the outset as this Blackburn Shark torpedo-bomber of 820 Squadron flying down the starboard side of HMS *Courageous.*
[VIA R. C. JONES

Above: The Shark doubled up as a floatplane, principally for floatplane training at Lee-on-Solent as here. [CDR MCTURK

Above: By the time of the Royal Review at Spithead in 1937 the Swordfish was well-established in service forming a large part of the fly-past. Here Swordfishes pass the Royal Yacht *Victoria & Albert* with a 'Nelson' class battleship beyond.
[THE AEROPLANE

Top right: Competitor to the Shark was another biplane, the Fairey TSR2, ordered and named the Swordfish. It entered service in July 1936. It very quickly entered and, as can be seen from HMS *Glorious*'s deck, gave the carriers a common torpedo and spotter aircraft in numbers. [R. MASSON/R. C. JONES

Right: Another important aircraft that entered service concurrently with the Swordfish was the Supermarine Walrus amphibian. Developed from a line of 'Seagull' amphibians the prototype being the Seagull V it became an indispensable tool for the Fleet Air Arm. Originally cast in a Fleet-Spotter-Recce role, it took on any task required, offensive or defensive and was to be found wherever RN ships appeared. Whilst it was used on aircraft-carriers as here on *Eagle* in 1937 (see following page—*top*) . . .
[VIA R. C. JONES

... its more normal habitat was aboard the ships of the various cruiser squadrons from which it was catapulted off and recovered as this sequence of shots shows. The aircraft shown is one belonging to HMS *Manchester*. The pilot first taxies alongside the ship whilst a hapless crew member poises himself on the upper wing a foot or two forward of the pusher propeller. [CDR MCTURK
Middle left/Bottom left: Having stabilised himself, he reaches out from the line dangling from the ship's derrick and secures it to the top wing. The engine is shut down ...
[CDR MCTURK
... and the Walrus is peacefully hoisted aboard. [CDR MCTURK

Top: In 1938 an important ship joined the Fleet in the shape of HMS *Ark Royal*. The biggest and best British carrier to date she was equipped with a full complement of the Navy's latest aircraft. In this photograph of an 810 Squadron Swordfish banking over the *Ark Royal*, the general arrangement of the ship can be clearly seen with the deck lifts, the two catapults forward and the landing circle aft.
Above: Amongst the new aircraft serving on *Ark Royal* was the Blackburn Skua divebomber, the first monoplane with retractable undercarriage, two of which are seen leaving the ship's port catapult.
[VIA R. C. JONES

Top: Skuas of *Ark Royal*'s 803 Squadron flying off the Isle of Wight coast in 1939. The Skuas doubled up as fighters in the early days of the War and it was one of 803 Squadron's aircraft which shot down the first enemy aircraft, a Dornier DO18 flying-boat, to fall to a British aircraft in World War Two. [AEROPLANE PHOTO SUPPLY

Above: The new fighter which entered FAA service just before World War II was still a biplane, a navalised version of the RAF's Gloster Gladiator named, not surprisingly, the Sea Gladiator. No 801 Squadron (*Courageous*) was the first front-line squadron to fly them but, although they did good work in small numbers from the carriers they were obsolescent before they even entered service and soon had to be superseded. This aircraft, the first production Sea Gladiator, is shown as part of No 801 Squadron at Evanton on the eve World War II with a Blackburn Skua, the aircraft which replaced it in 801 Squadron. [J. M. BRUEN

Above: In the last years of peace one of the Navy's perennial tasks, showing the flag around the world, was also carried out by the FAA. Two of HMS *Manchester*'s Supermarine Walruses with White Ensigns akimbo, and topee-ed crew impress 'the natives of Mafia in June 1939. [CDR MCTURK

Below: As War broke out the carriers of the Fleet were out on anti-submarine patrol. HMS *Eagle* was on station in the Indian Ocean as witnessed by this observer's eye-view from a Swordfish taking off. Note the destroyer on 'plane guard' duties on the port quarter. [T. SPEARIE/R. C. JONES

Top/Above: One of the urgent tasks of the Fleet Air Arm during the 'Phoney War' period was to train more and more personnel. The Naval Fighter School (No 759 Squadron) was based at Eastleigh at this time and was training pilots on the Sea Gladiator . . . [CAPT P. S. C. CHILTON

. . . and the Blackburn Roc, a development of the Skua with a 4-gun turret which slowed the aircraft down so much as to make it almost a non-starter. [CAPT P. C. S. CHILTON

Top/Above: Norway was the Fleet Air Arm's first campaign in World War II; it was here that the Blackburn Skua squadrons were in evidence, either flying from Hatston in the Orkneys . . .
[J. HINDLEY VIA R. C. JONES

. . . or from the snow and ice of Norway itself, viz this 801 Squadron aircraft under the quizzical eyes of Norwegian soldiers.
[VIA R. C. JONES

Top: Fighter cover in the Norwegian campaign was largely in the hands of the Sea Gladiators, principally 804 Squadron from *Glorious* one of whose aircraft is seen here on lonely patrol. [CAPT P. C. S. CHILTON

Above: HMS *Glorious* one of the two *Courageous* class carriers served for some months off Norway before succumbing with fearful loss of life. [VIA M. MCEVOY

Above: The backbone on the Navy's carrier force in World War II and immediately after was the 'Illustrious' class of Fleet carrier. HMS *Illustrious* herself was the first to be commissioned, and it was this ship that became the stage for that most famous of all Fleet Air Arm actions, Taranto. From her deck twenty-one Swordfish set off by night and crippled a major part of the Italian Fleet. Here she is seen, about Taranto time, recovering her Swordfish with one stowed forward of the barrier, one approaching to land over the round-down, one about to turn into her landing circuit and one joining. [IWM

Below: The weapon system which effected such havoc at Taranto was simply the torpedo-equipped Swordfish (this one, an 812 Squadron aircraft). [A. W. JOLLY

Top: The Walrus continued to play a diverse and effective role in many parts of the world from the South Atlantic to the Arctic, wherever ships with catapults went. Sitting on a catapult with engine running this aircraft shows the wartime configuration with gun hatches closed (they were rarely used), ASV aerials on the forward interplane struts. [IWM

Above: The advent of *Illustrious* had brought a new Fleet fighter to the scene. This was the Fairey Fulmar which, whilst an improvement on previous fighters, was still too slow being a converted bomber. *Ark Royal* also took Fulmars to the Mediterranean (808 Squadron) a flight of whose aircraft we see here. [M. B. WARBECK-HOWELL VIA R. C. JONES

Top: The defeat of the *Bismarck* would hardly have taken place were it not for Fleet Air Arm aircraft. Her escape was detected by a Maryland from 771 Squadron at Hatston, a rather improbable aircraft to be used by the FAA. This historic photograph shows HM King George VI inspecting the Squadron after the event with the Maryland in the background [CDR MCTURK

Above: The *Bismarck's* flight was halted by a judicious torpedo strike from *Ark Royal's* Swordfish. K8375 was one of 810 Squadron's aircraft aboard *Ark Royal* used on the strike. [VIA R. C. JONES

Top: When American aircraft became available, the Fleet Air Arm tapped this source to help solve its equipment problems. Not all purchases were successful; the Vought-Sikorsky Chesapeake equipped 811 Squadron at Lee-on-Solent as a dive-bomber but the type went no further. [CDR MCTURK

Above/Top right: Several FAA fighter units found themselves ashore in Egypt in 1941 with little prospect of carrier action. They formed a Naval Fighter Wing which threw itself into the desert battle alongside the RAF. Prominent was 805 Squadron which soldiered on with Gladiators and Brewster Buffaloes . . .
[CAPT P. S. C. CHILTON

... until the Martlet arrived with which the Squadron thrived. [CAPT P. S. C. CHILTON

Above: When 805 Squadron moved to East Africa it had, as transport aircraft, the ancient French Farman in the background.
[CAPT P. S. C. CHILTON

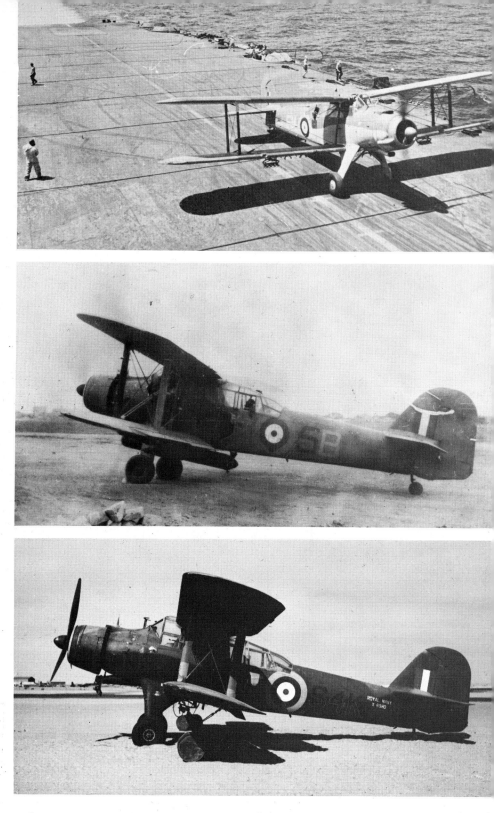

Top left: Just before the War began a replacement for the Fairey Swordfish appeared. Named the Albacore it had a Taurus sleeve-valve engine and enclosed cockpits for the crew. Coming into service in 1940 it was mainly used as a torpedo-bomber whilst afloat. Here X9157 '5M' of 820 Squadron is arrested by the first of *Victorious* wires and taxies forward whilst the next aircraft appears over the round-down. [IWM

Middle left: But the Albacore was by no means confined to carrier operations and will always be remembered for its work in the Mediterranean from Malta. This aircraft, X8942 of 828 Squadron is taxying out from Hal Far for shipping strike.
[W. N. JONES VIA R. C. JONES

Left: The Albacore also served in the desert battles flying with the RAF's night bombers acting in a pathfinder role (was this where the RAF's idea came from?) flying ahead and dropping flares on the Libyan ports. 815 and 826 were the squadrons that carried out this task. [HOWARD LEVY

Above: 1941 saw the Fleet at last receiving fighters which could take on hostile air forces. The Hurricane had been navalised and quite apart from the catapult flights was taken aboard the fleet carriers. The flight deck of *Indomitable* is interesting in showing the new equipment in service with a Sea Hurricane in the foreground, a Swordfish and Albacore astern and a Martlet being brought up the rear lift. Astern is HMS *Eagle* with Fulmars on her deck. [IWM

Top: The Sea Hurricane on the carrier did not have folding wings so they posed handling problems as can be seen in this photo of *Argus* hangar with but a few aircraft filling the space. [E. A. HARLIN
Above: Second-line duties in the Fleet Air Arm continued to increase and a miscellany of aircraft performed this task.

The Blackburn Roc which had been a mediocre fighter, found a new lease of life as a target tug, towing targets for the Fleet's guns to practise on. 771 Squadron was one of the Fleet Requirement Units which carried out this and other tasks in many places, this Roc flying from Hatston in the Orkneys. [L. J. KELLY VIA R. C. JONES

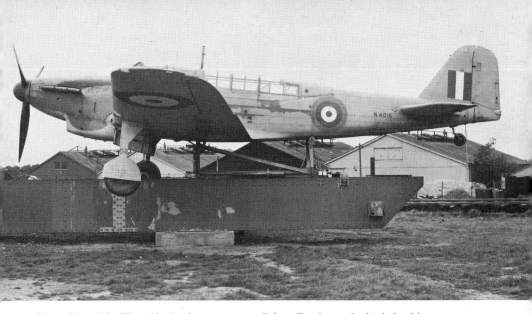

Above: One of the Fleet Air Arm's good allies has been the Royal Aircraft Establishment at Farnborough. This has given a helping hand with many of the problems of naval flying, not least in the development of effective catapults. This Fairey Fulmar is mounted on the catapult which was a familiar piece of RAE furniture in the thirties and forties.

Below: Farnborough also helped in weapon development. One project which never came to fruition was the Toraplane; developed in conjunction with the Torpedo Development Unit at Gosport, it was a torpedo with wings and a tailplane, the intention being to overcome the danger of flying close to the target.

Top left: Argus the first real carrier, was still busy through the war years as a training ship, accepting many different types for deck-landing practice. Even the Swordfish could have troubles as this pilot from Crail found. [CDR MCTURK

Left: Victorious was involved in supporting the Russian Front in the summer of 1941 by mounting attacks on Northern Norway. She is seen here in Sandefjord with an 809 Sqdn

Fulmar aboard. [VIA R. C. JONES

Above: In 1941 the Fleet decided it must have Spitfires. So Cdr H. P. Bramwell, DSO, DSC took a 'hooked' Spitfire VB aboard HMS *Illustrious* in November for deck trials. This success heralded the onset of a line of Supermarine Seafire fighters which played a considerable part in the later war operations. [IWM

Top left/Middle left: The catapult flights
continued to operate on through the War.
Malaya's Swordfish is being lowered,
with engine running, for a water-borne
take-off . . .

. . . and *Warspite*'s Walrus is hoisted aboard.
[VIA R. C. JONES

Left: Another floatplane joined the FAA in
1942, the Vought-Sikorsky Kingfisher which
was used both for training, where its

single-float provided a useful variation on the
theme, and operationally with 703 Squadron
aboard Armed Merchant Cruisers. FN696
Seumas served aboard *Corfu*. [K. R. LOWN
Top/Above: Corfu was a converted P&O ship
and had accommodation aft for the
Kingfisher . . .
[K. R. LOWN
. . . which was somewhat limited (this is
aboard another AMC *Cilicia*). [R. C. JONES

Above: The Kingfisher was used mainly for observation although it had bomb racks and two machine-guns. This is *Brenda* with HMS *Corfu* in the background. [K. R. LOWN

Below: The floatplanes were picked up by taxying on to this mat and then the crew members coming forward to engage the line lowered from the winch. (FN709 joining *Cilicia*). [VIA B. J. LOWE

Above: The traditional naval manufacturers were busy in the mid-years developing new naval aircraft. Fairey were developing the Barracuda as a Swordfish/Albacore replacement. The prototype appeared at one stage with a fixed undercarriage as here at Boscombe Down. [P. M. MOSS

Below/Bottom: Blackburns were struggling with the Firebrand, a new naval concept of a fighter which could also carry a torpedo . . . [VIA A. J. TODD

. . . it was plagued by engine troubles (Napier Sabre) and eventually was re-engined and entered service after the War. [D. ANDREOLI VIA R. C. JONES

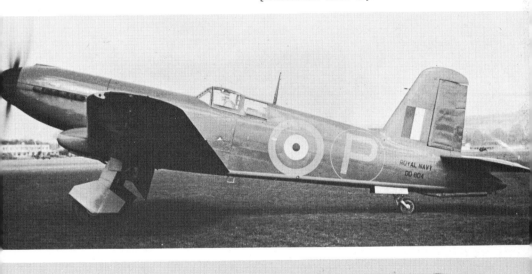

Top: The most significant factor in the anti-submarine offensive in the middle years of the war was the advent of the Escort Carriers, the small Woolworth carrier produced in the US and in the UK. These, equipped with a few Swordfish and Wildcats, sailed with the convoys and by keeping the U-boat heads down or destroyed, achieved a worthwhile reduction in losses. (HMS *Battler* with five Swordfish ranged aft.) [K. R. LOWN

Above: Take-off view of *Battler* shows the general deck arrangement and emphasises the lack of room for error in flying on and off. [K. R. LOWN

Top: It has been a penchant of the Fleet Air Arm to enter into minor wars and campaigns despite the purely naval significance. When the Madagascan campaign began the Fleet Air Arm training squadron in East Africa No 796, operated from Tanga with its Albatross (BF588 here) with great gusto, joining the carrier aircraft. [P. HOUSDEN *Above:* Also at Madagascar was HMS *Formidable*, flying off a Fulmar of 803 Squadron for a patrol. HMS *Valiant* is off the port bow. [VIA R. C. JONES

Below: It then went ashore to La Senia airfield, Oran, where it flew coastal patrols. [VIA R. C. JONES

Bottom: Operation 'Torch' was to see the FAA in strength with seven carriers present for the landings in North Africa (*Formidable, Victorious, Furious, Biter, Dasher, Argus* and *Avenger*). 820 Squadron on *Formidable* flew day and night, dive-bombed Algiers and sank a U-boat. [VIA PETER ARNOLD

Right: It was during Operation 'Torch' that the Seafire, navalised Spitfire, made its debut, 885 Squadron flying six aboard *Formidable* (seen here) and *Furious* carrying twenty divided between 801 and 807 Squadrons. [IWM

Bottom right: The Seafire's first victory was this Dewoitine D.520 which attempted to interfere with a strike on La Senia airfield and was shot down by Lt (now Capt) G. C. Baldwin, DSC, RN. [MOD

Top left: In the main the Fleet Air Arm had been using the same weapons with which it opened the War. In 1943 however a new weapon came into operation, fitting on to any aircraft. It was the air-launched 'Rocket projectile' and the evergreen 'Stringbag' could carry four under each wing. This made a formidable new antagonist for U-boats; an aircraft from *Archer*'s 819 Squadron destroying one. [J. CULSHAW

Middle left/Bottom left: The FAA training organisation had by 1943 grown world-wide. At home it was using aircraft acquired from the RAF—Tiger Moths with 780 Squadron at Lee-on-Solent . . .
[L. J. KELLY VIA R. C. JONES

. . . and Westland Lysander target-tugs and for air-gunnery training with 773 Squadron at Worthy Down. [VIA R. C. JONES

Above: To supplement the escort carriers, arriving all too slowly, came the MAC ships, Merchant Aircraft Carriers, which were merchant ships with superstructures cut down and a flight deck put on top. In this they followed the layout of the perennial *Argus.*

Top: In South Africa 789 Squadron was an
Operational Training Unit at Wingfield,
Cape Town. [J. E. J. BAGGS VIA R. C. JONES
Centre: Whilst in the West Indies a big
Observer training station was established at
Piarco, Trinidad with the Percival Proctor,
Grumman Goose (here) and Stinson Reliant.

[A. Y. BALFOUR VIA R. C. JONES
Above: 'The Barracuda was, in appearance,
distinctly odd'. It entered service in 1943 and
fought from the Fleet carriers for the rest of
the War. This aircraft flew on training
duties with 711 Squadron at Crail.
[A. I. STANBRIDGE VIA R. C. JONES

Above: HMS *Unicorn* was something rather one-off amongst carriers during the War. It was built as a Maintenance Carrier serving in the supply and repair role and also in transporting aircraft from the UK to operational areas. However, at the Salerno beachhead she took on an operational role with three and a half Squadrons of Seafires aboard. [VIA J. DAWES

Below: At the Salerno landings the Seafire was the key aircraft. One hundred and fifteen were ranged on five escort carriers to provide massive air cover and for three days the Seafires did just this; but at the end only twenty-six remained serviceable due, not to enemy action, but to the aircraft's skittishness on the flight deck as evidenced by this barrier prang by an 807 Squadron Seafire on HMS *Battler* at Salerno. [MOD

Above/Below: This problem of deck landing plagued the Seafire for the rest of its carrier-borne days. Some just managed to stay on board. . .
[CDR MCTURK

. . . Others were not that lucky.
[VIA PETER ARNOLD

Top: Until the mid-war years little had been done to provide the Fleet with adequate night-fighters but developments with fitting the Fulmar II with AI (note aerials above and below the wingtips) in 1943 led to its introduction into squadron service (No 784 at Drem) early in 1944 and operationally with 813 Squadron later that year.
[T. LITTLE VIA R. C. JONES

Above: With the somewhat unsatisfactory position of new British naval aircraft development in 1943 the Navy looked to the US for suitable equipment, the first successful purchase (apart from the Martlet/Wildcat already established in service) was the Grumman Avenger, a torpedo-bomber which could also use other forms of weaponry. Many squadrons were formed and worked up in the United States, flew across by carrier providing convoy cover, and then into action. Typical of these was 846 Squadron, formed at Quonset in April 1943, which flew across to Hatston on HMS *Ravager.* [P. HOUSDEN

Above: Although the sea war moved its emphasis eastwards in 1944, there remained the everlasting job of convoy escort. The MAC ships soldiered on at this task, No 836 Squadron providing the aircraft and crews, two on a converted tanker, four on a grain ship. This photograph of H Flight aboard the *Empire McAndrew* in February, 1944 epitomises the cold misery of such operations.

Left: The conditions for the flight deck were not always as bad. This Swordfish is being started aboard *Unicorn* by means of the time-honoured starting handle whilst the observer settles himself in the rear cockpit. Of interest is the early ASV aerial on the upper wing leading edge. [VIA J. DAWES

Top right: In early April 1944 the Fleet Air Arm set out to attack the last remaining German capital ship *Tirpitz* in Kaa Fjord, Norway. The largest carrier in the force was *Victorious* here seen encountering heavy weather off Norway. Together with *Furious* she carried the main strike force totalling forty-two Barracudas. [K. R. LOWN

Middle right: Three Escort carriers supplied fighter cover of which *Emperor* carried two squadrons of Grumman Hellcats, Nos 800 and 804.

Right: The Barracudas of 52 TBR Wing en route for Kaa Fjord and the *Tirpitz*, April 3rd, 1944. [VIA K. R. LOWN

Top: The bombs from the Barracudas hit *Tirpitz.* [K. R. LOWN
Above: Another new American fighter which appeared operationally for the first time on the *Tirpitz* attack was the Vought Corsair, distinguished by its inverted gull-wing and ruggedness. Two squadrons were aboard *Victorious.* [CAPT P. C. S. CHILTON

Top/Above: One American aircraft which never developed far in FAA service was the Curtiss Helldiver. One Squadron, No 1820, formed in April, 1944 (note the squadron badge on the nose of JW110) . . . [E. B. EVERETT

. . . and embarked on HMS *Arbiter* in July, 1944 for the UK but saw no further operational service. [E. B. EVERETT

Top left: The Swordfish remained irrespressible. As the MkIII it was fitted with a large ASV radome between the undercarriage legs and bombs under the wings. It flew a highly individualistic and successful war from Manston along the Continental coast on German E-boats. Together with some Albacores one squadron (No 841) transferred to the Royal Canadian Air Force on this task. [VIA R. C. JONES

Middle left: The other Manston Squadron, No 819, carried on the good work up to and beyond D-Day. [J. CULSHAW

Left: It was this Squadron, 819, whose antiquated Swordfish flew over the invasion fleet on D-Day, covering them with smoke-screens. [J. CULSHAW

Top/Above: To fulfill its second-line needs the Navy continued to acquire ex-RAF types. This Defiant served with 792 Squadron at St. Merryn for target-towing duties . . .
[K. ATKINSON VIA R. C. JONES

. . . whilst this Beaufighter II was one of a number which the Fleet Air Arm's 775 Squadron used on Fleet Requirement duties around the Mediterranean. [J. DAWES

Above: The final FAA operations in the Mediterranean took place in September, 1944 in the Aegean Sea. Prominent in these was HMS *Emperor* with the two dozen Hellcats of 800 Squadron aboard.

Below: Frantic activity as the deck crew manoeuvre Hellcat 'L' into position for take-off from *Emperor*.

Above: Towards the end of 1944 came the migration of the carrier force to the Pacific. HMS *Stalker* with Seafires of 807 and 809 Squadrons aboard (and an odd Harvard) is followed through the Suez Canal by another Escort Carrier. [D. D. JAMES VIA M. GARBETT

Below: The Fairey Firefly two-seat fighter came into service in 1944, the first Squadron, No 1770, going aboard HMS *Indefatigable* in home waters before following the general exodus eastwards at the end of the year. 820 Squadron Barracudas are ranged astern of the Fireflies and both squadrons took part in operation 'Goodwood' and strikes in Norwegian waters. [HOGGARD

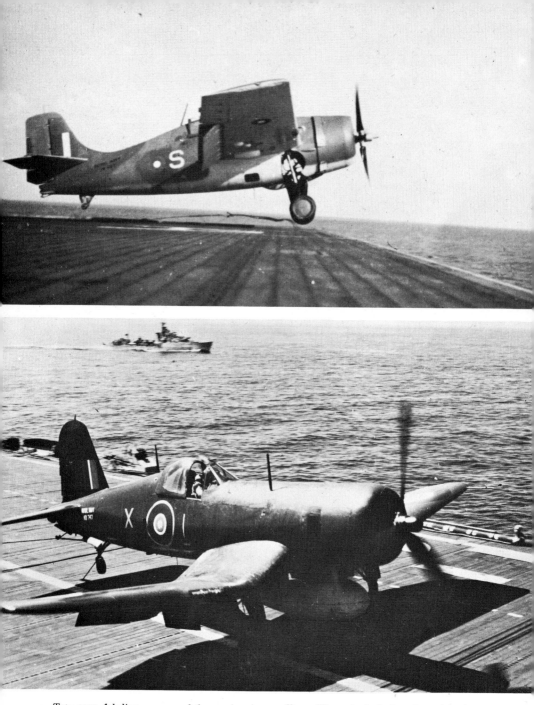

Top: HMS *Atheling* was one of the carriers in the early build-up of the Fleet in the Indian Ocean and served as a fighter escort carrier with one squadron of Seafires (889) and one of Wildcats (890). JV435, of 890 Squadron seen at the point of departure, going off the bows of *Atheling* with the catapult strop falling away. [E. J. T. NEWCOMB

Above: The principal aircraft used in the Fleet Air Arm in the Pacific were the new generation of American aircraft—the Vought Corsair in this case KD747 of 1843 Squadron taking the wire on HMS *Arbiter* crossing from America to Australia. [CAPT P. C. S. CHILTON

Top: The Grumman Hellcat served both in the pure fighter and in the strike role.
[J. HINDLEY VIA R. C. JONES

Above: The Grumman Avenger provided the main weight of bombs. An 854 Sqdn aircraft takes off from HMS *Indomitable* in the Indian Ocean. [D. JENKINS VIA R. C. JONES

158

Top left: Probably the most significant contribution the Royal Navy made towards the completion of the war in the Far East was carried out by two strikes, on January 24th and 29th, 1945 on oil refineries at Pledjoe and Soengi Gerong, Palembang. These reduced the output of oil to 35 per cent of its normal production. Smoke rises as a result of 820 Squadron's Avengers' bombs. [HOGGARD

Left: Striking nearer the heart of Japan. Task Force 57, the British Pacific Fleet, working with the US Navy, attacked airfields on the islands of the Sakishima Gunto in April, 1945. *Indomitable*'s 857 Squadron flies in over Ishyaki Island to strike.
[A. H. HURST VIA R. C. JONES

Above: The CO of *Indomitable*'s 1839 Squadron, Lt Cdr D. Jenkins, enters the barrier on return from a strike in the Sakishima Gunto. The aircraft was virtually undamaged. [D. JENKINS VIA R. C. JONES

Right: This Hellcat of 808 Squadron on *Khedive* was less fortunate; note the fuselage buckling behind the cockpit. [VIA R. C. JONES

Below: And the pilot of this 1843 Squadron Corsair broke his neck—but recovered.
[CAPT P. C. S. CHILTON

Above: The Fleet Air Arm's last European blow was on May 4th, 1945 at Kilboltn near Hastad when Avengers and Wildcats from *Queen, Searcher* and *Trumpeter* sank a U-boat depot ship

Top right: As the War in Europe drew to a close the convoy work carried on. It was still hazardous as is evident from this episode on *Campania*—note the deck crew running to assist despite the bomb wedged between the wing and the deck and the aircrew hastily evacuating. [T. LITTLE VIA R. C. JONES

Middle right: Whilst the Fleet Carriers were busy in the Pacific the Escorts were in the winding-up stage in Malaya. A Hellcat from 896 Squadron on *Empress* is ready to be catapulted for a rocket strike in August, 1945. [J. W. G. WELHAM VIA R. C. JONES

Right: For the final operations of the War *Indefatigable* acquired a second Firefly Squadron, No 1772. Even on this modern aircraft wing-folding made use of many hands. Four rockets were carried under each wing. [K. R. LOWN

Above: Even Fireflies had barrier problems.
[K. R. LOWN

Below: Before the War ended a prophetic sight appeared aboard RN ships—their first helicopter. These were Vought-Sikorsky Hoverfly I's, a small batch bought for the RAF and FAA to use for experiments and development.

Above/Below: Reinforcements were moving steadily to the Pacific and as the War came to a close were all over the globe, for example HMS *Colossus*, one of the new Light Fleet Carriers, was exercising its carrier Air Group over Cape Town, South Africa. It comprised No 827 Squadron with Barracudas . . . [R. C. JONES

. . . and 1846 Squadron with Corsairs. [R. C. JONES

Above: On September 10th, 1945 HMS *Emperor* ceremonially entered Singapore Harbour, 800 Squadron's Hellcats ranged on the flight deck which was lined by Jolly Jacks. [N. S. PAINTER VIA R. C. JONES

Below: With the onset of peace the Navy soon settled into a system of using two types of aircraft carriers, the Fleet carriers, exemplified here by HMS *Implacable* and the Light Fleet Carriers with HMS *Vengeance* in the foreground. Both are at anchor in Weymouth Bay. The wartime Escorts and MAC ships soon disappeared. [CHARLES E. BROWN

Above: Their basic equipment was still the Firefly FR1 and Seafire, now a Griffon-engined variant the F15 and F17. Ranged on HMS *Vengeance*'s deck are 802 Squadron with Seafire F15s and 814 Squadron with Firefly FR1s. [VIA B. J. LOWE

Below: With the almost overnight disappearance of American aircraft the Fleet Air Arm looked to the British aircraft industry to make up the gaps. Faireys developed the Barracuda to an even higher degree in the Mark V although it soon faded from the scene seeing little service, and that in second-line squadrons as here with 783 Squadron. [A. J. STANBRIDGE VIA R. C. JONES

Top: Faireys decided to concentrate on the Firefly, producing a substantial re-design with the Mk IV prototype.
Above: Supermarine developed a successor to the ubiquitous Walrus in the Sea Otter but this never achieved the same success as the Walrus for there were now few catapult slips. It mainly served as a 'tilly' at various Air Stations and aboard carriers. This aircraft is RD 881 *Virginia*, station hack at St Merryn paying a visit to nearby St Eval in 1947. [AUTHOR

Top: Blackburn had spent the whole war developing the Firebrand. Eventually re-engined with a Bristol Centaurus radial, it was ready for service in its TF4 version.

Above: The Firebrand entered service in September, 1945, the month that World War II ended, and spent a lengthy work-up at Ford with 813 Squadron.

Top: Re-equipped with the final Firebrand variant, the TF5, 813 Squadron went aboard HMS *Implacable* in 1948 but the Firebrand was not a good aircraft on carrier decks. A further squadron, 827, flew them on *Eagle* in the early fifties.
[LT CDR BROWN VIA R. C. JONES

Above: For long-range fighter duties de Havilland developed the Sea Mosquito TR33. It served with No 811 Squadron at Ford but never went to sea, being overtaken by another aircraft from the same stable, the Sea Hornet. [VIA A. J. TODD

Top: The most successful Fleet fighter to emanate immediately after the war was the Hawker Sea Fury and this type began a decade of service in August, 1947. 802 Squadron was the first to receive Sea Furies and it took these to Cape Town as part of 15th Carrier Air Group in HMS *Vengeance* during the Royal visit to South Africa in the winter of 1948. [VIA B. J. LOWE

Above: The de Havilland Sea Hornet F20 was developed from the Hornet for the RAF as a long-range fighter for the Fleet Air Arm. It served aboard HMS *Implacable* with 801 Squadron with some success and also formed part of an aerobatic display squadron, No 806, which toured the US and Canada in 1948 showing them how aerobatics should be performed. TT209 was one of 801 Squadron's aircraft loaned to 806 for the tour. [HOWARD LEVY VIA AUTHOR

Above: But the new Fleet Air Arm would sooner or later have to become jet-powered. In fact, HMS *Ocean*, a light Fleet carrier, witnessed the very first carrier launching by a jet-aircraft in the world when, on December 4th, 1945, Lt Cdr E. M. 'Winkle' Bown landed the prototype Sea Vampire, LZ551. [CHARLES E. BROWN

Below: The first carrier jet for the Navy was the Supermarine Attacker. Prototype trials took place aboard HMS *Illustrious* in October 1947

Top: As successor to the Firebrand Westland produced the Wyvern but had the misfortune to choose the Rolls-Royce Eagle piston-engine. This was very troublesome and took a high toll in prototypes, this aircraft TS371 crashing fatally a few minutes after this photograph was taken. [THE AEROPLANE

Middle: This was followed by the order of a small production batch of Sea Vampire F20s which, though they never went to sea, performed a vital function in teaching the Fleet Air Arm about jet aircraft characteristics and tactics. VV139 served with 703 Squadron and is here lined up on Ford's runway. [AUTHOR

Above: Although the Fleet Air Arm had experimented with a few Hoverflies in 1945/47 it began to cut its helicopter teeth on the Dragonfly which was used at Gosport by 705 Squadron for helicopter training and by various Air Stations as Station Flight aircraft. Here they were called upon to carry out rescue duties. At Ford Lt Cdr J. S. Sproule developed a scoop net for use from his Dragonfly to pick people out of the sea. [MOD

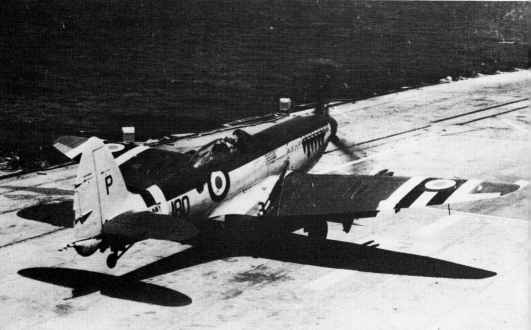

Top: Experiments were carried out on an old wartime Victory ship the *Fort Duquesne,* to assess the practicability of landing helicopters on merchant ships. But this was in advance of its time. [PA-REUTER

Above: The Korean War caught the world by surprise. The Navy had HMS *Triumph,* a Light Fleet Carrier, in the Far East and she was deployed to the Korean War with Seafires and Fireflies. The Seafires operated by 800 Squadron, were the last version, the F47, one of which is seen here taking off from *Triumph* with RATOG gear fitted but not yet fired! [IWM

Top: Within two months HMS *Theseus* had been readied and sailed from Portsmouth with the 17th Carrier Air Group aboard comprising 807 Squadron with Sea Furies and 810 Squadron with Firefly FR5s. [PA-REUTER

Above: Despite conditions reminiscent of the Russian convoys *Theseus* kept her aircraft flying whenever possible. [MOD

Top: 810 Squadron Fireflies return to *Theseus* with hooks down. [VIA G. J. THOMAS
Middle: An 807 Squadron Sea Fury FB1 lands in over the round-down of *Theseus.* [VIA G. J. THOMAS

Above: The sea Fury/Firefly formula had proved successful and the Royal Australian Navy, similarly equipped, brought HMAS *Sydney* into the Korean theatre. She borrowed a helicopter from the US Navy for rescue duties. [IWM

Above: In the early fifties the Naval Air Days became popular institutions when the various Air Stations opened their gates to the public. This is Bramcote circa 1952 showing a static park of mainly piston-engined aircraft apart from the Sea Vampire and the Meteor T7 borrowed from the RAF. [VIA B. J. LOWE

Below: In 1952 the second aircraft-carrier by the name of HMS *Eagle* was commissioned. The biggest yet, she also became the first in the Royal Navy to operate a squadron of jet fighters, No 800 Squadron with Attackers. The aircraft that can be seen on her deck, however, are Firebrand TF5s of 827 Squadron.

Top left: An Attacker F1, WA531, of 800 Squadron taxying forward on HMS *Eagle* after landing-on.

Middle left: Despite all these advances the carriers were still basically the same in configuration as at the beginning of World War II. But advances were just around the corner which would render impossible the sort of costly accident epitomised by this tragedy aboard HMAS *Sydney* where a Firefly is sailing over the barrier, seconds off crunching into the aircraft taxying just ahead of it. [WILLIAMS VIA R. C. JONES

Left: Getting airborne in a hurry from Ford were *Eagle*'s two squadrons of Attackers 800 and 803. [AUTHOR

Above: Her Majesty's review of her Fleet in 1953 took place in the midst of the transition from the old (in terms of piston-engined aircraft) to the new (jets and helicopters). To put up the mammoth flypast of 279 aircraft both Lee-on-Solent and Ford were used. Seventy Fireflies and Sea Furies, engines running, prepare to take-off from Ford's runway. [MOD

Right: Leading the fly-past were helicopters from 705 Squadron at Gosport, a Hiller HTE2, a Dragonfly HR3 and the prototype Whirlwind. Beneath them can be seen the fixed-wing line-up on Lee's runway, including some Grumman Avengers, re-purchased to fill a gap in the anti-submarine role. [AUTHOR

Right: The Whirlwind had come to stay with the Fleet Air Arm and already a squadron had been fitted out and sent to Malaya. No 848, flying American-built Whirlwinds, entered into the Malayan jungle conflict in 1953 and, forgetting about ship work, hammered out techniques under strenuous operational conditions for all the British services. [THE AEROPLANE

Below: The Sea Hornet had been developed into a two-seat night-fighter in the NF21, a version which gave yeoman service in developing a night-fighter concept in the Navy. 809 was the operational squadron using the NF21. [FLIGHT

Bottom: 809 operated aboard several carriers (*Indomitable* in this case) not always with complete success. [VIA B. J. LOWE

Above: From the original Eagle-engined Wyvern was developed a version re-engined with the Armstrong-Siddeley Python turbo-prop. This entered service as a Firebrand replacement equipping four squadrons in all. 813 Squadron was the first with Wyverns, flying them aboard HMS *Eagle*; in this configuration they are carrying additional long-range tanks on the fuselage weapon pylon. [VIA B. J. LOWE

Below: In the mid-fifties the Fleet Air Arm took up a new concept, that of Airborne Early Warning. Aircraft equipped with large radar would fly ahead of the Fleet picking up any hostile activity over the horizon. The US Navy had pioneered this concept and it was American aircraft, Douglas Skyraiders, which formed the Fleet Air Arm's first operational AEW Squadron, No 849, which deployed flights to each carrier.

Top: As well as being a torpedo aircraft the Wyvern was also handy with rockets, as was proved later at Suez. [MOD

Above: Although the Attacker was the Navy's first jet fighter to go to sea it was the Hawker Sea Hawk which became the standard fighter of the Fleet Air Arm, a beautiful aircraft, delightful to fly and handy for hanging all manner of weaponry underneath. The first squadron No 806, formed under the command of Lt Cdr Pat Chilton in March, 1953, carried the 'Ace of Diamonds' as its motif.

Top: The mid-fifties saw the introduction of a completely new generation of Fleet Air Arm aircraft; coming rather later than intended, the Fairey Gannet took up the anti-submarine role. It was a 3-seater with retractable radar aft of the capacious weapons bay in the fuselage; visible under the wings are rocket rails for use in softening-up a target during attack. This particular aircraft carries the Watney's Harp and black and white spinners of 815 Squadron. [AUTHOR

Above: Benefitting from the work of the night-fighter Sea Hornets, a radar-equipped all-weather fighter force became a reality for the carriers with the advent of the de Havilland Sea Venom. 891 Squadron, formed in 1954, emblazoned their aircraft with their Tiki badge, seen here on Ford's runway. [AUTHOR

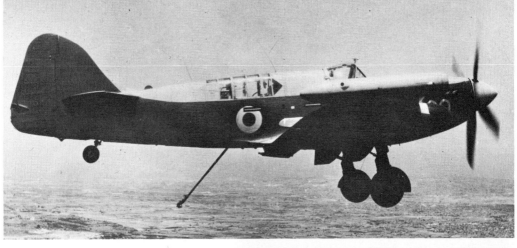

Left: The first British carrier to incorporate Captain Campbell's angled deck, answer to all the barrier and deck accidents, was the light fleet carrier HMS *Centaur* seen here off Australia during a replenishment at sea exercise with the Fleet Oiler RFA *Tidesurge* and destroyer HMS *Lagos*. By steaming on a parallel course at 20 knots the oiler can replenish both *Centaur* and *Lagos* simultaneously enabling the vessels to remain at sea over long periods. Overhead is a Gannet from 810 Squadron.

Bottom left: As well as the front-line operations the Fleet Air Arm has always needed many second-line activities. One type which served the Navy well for a long time in the communications role was the de Havilland Dominie, alias the pre-war Dragon Rapide, which stayed in service until finally ousted by the helicopter in the late fifties. [AUTHOR

Above: With the advent of the Gannet the Firefly became surplus. A number of these were converted into drones, and, painted red and yellow, were flown to be shot at by the Fleet. Many of them, as this one, were based with 727 Squadron at Hal Far in Malta to which this aircraft is making a pilotless approach.

Right: Whatever else the Suez affair did it gave striking confirmation of the rightness and effectiveness of the FAA's carrier force. The Fleet Carrier *Eagle* steams into action showing clearly the post-war innovations which had revolutionised carrier operations the angled deck, the mirror-landing sight, outboard on the port side adjacent with the Sea Hawks and the steam catapult forward. [VIA B. J. LOWE

Above: 830 Squadron's bomb-laden Wyverns marshal forward on *Eagle* preparatory for a strike on the Canal Zone. Note the AEW Skyraiders aft and the destroyer on 'plane guard' duties.

Below/Right: 830's Wyverns hit Dekheila airfield . . .
[VIA R. C. JONES
. . . and oil installations. [VIA R. C. JONES

Above: Fighter cover had to be provided by the Sea Hawks and Sea Venoms of the Fleet as the Cyprus-based Hunters of the RAF had insufficient range. *Bulwark* swings into wind as the Sea Hawks of 804 Squadron taxi forward to the catapult.
[M. W. STARMER VIA R. C. JONES

Below: Advanced radar cover was provided by the Skyraiders of 849 Squadron, this aircraft making a non-catapult take-off from the angled deck of HMS *Albion*. Note the black and yellow stripes painted on participating aircraft. [MOD

Top: A Sea Venom sinks momentarily after catapulting off *Bulwark* for a Suez operation. [M. W. STARMER VIA R. C. JONES

Middle: One of the unspectacular but worthwhile developments after the 1939–45 War had been the creation of the Air Branch of the RNVR. With squadrons in the Scottish, Midlands, London and South Coast areas they provided a naval equivalent to the Auxiliary Air Force. Originally Seafires predominated, as these Mk17s from 1832 Squadron at Culham. [AUTHOR

Above: The fighter squadrons of the RNVR graduated to Sea Furies—1833 Squadron flying from Bramcote. [D. JENKINS VIA R. C. JONES

Top left: With the development of dunking sonar the Fleet Air Arm decided to transfer its anti-submarine activities from the Gannet to the Whirlwind helicopter. The HAS7 version was produced capable of carrying torpedoes and mines and rushed into service. This aircraft, from 824 Squadron, HMS *Centaur*, is in its operational habitat low over the sea. [AUTHOR

Left: And finally to jets. An Attacker of the RNVR Wing taxies in at Benson against a stormy winter's sky. This Wing also received a few Sea Hawks but the whole Branch was axed soon afterwards in 1957. [AUTHOR

Bottom left: The Fleet Air Arm now jet-equipped did not rest on its laurels but pressed on towards the next generation of equipment. To assist in this the Naval Air Department of the RAE had taken up residence at its new airfield at Thurleigh, Beds. There, comprehensive layouts were made with catapults and arrester gear to simulate carrier decks so that new aircraft could be thoroughly tested before going afloat. One aircraft benefitting from this was the Supermarine N113, scheduled as the Fleet's transonic Sea Hawk replacement.

Above: The Whirlwind HAS7 also took over 'plane guard' duties from the destroyers. One of *Ark Royal*'s two SAR Whirlwinds lets down alongside the carrier level with the stern prior to recovering aircraft. [AUTHOR

Right: The end of the nineteen-fifties saw the Fleet Air Arm presenting aerobatic teams at the major air displays. 800 Squadron, practising here over Brawdy, took part in the 1958 SBAC Display at Farnborough. [THE AEROPLANE

Above: For the next generation of naval fighters air to air missiles were being developed in particular the Firestreak. Service tests were carried out by 703 Squadron at Ford whose Sea Venoms carried a Firestreak under each wing pylon. [AUTHOR
Below: The first aircraft to use this weapon operationally was the Sea Venom's successor, the de Havilland Sea Vixen FAW1. At last the Fleet Air Arm had a fighter which was comparable to any land-based fighter. This photograph of 893 Squadron's Sea Vixens being launched from *Centaur* gives a good idea of the method of high-speed launching in operation. The officer controlling the steam catapults is installed in the retractable cupola and has just released the Vixen on the port catapult which is approximately halfway along its take-off run. Already the next aircraft is taxying on to the star-board catapult, the flight deck crew marshalling him into position. Note the catapult strop laid across the slot forward of the retracted jet-blast deflector. The tractor is ready to assist marshalling. [AUTHOR

Top: End of a sortie. A Sea Vixen FAW1 of 890 Squadron beautifully placed over the round-down of *Ark Royal,* as seen from the Ship's Flight Whirlwind on plane duty. [AUTHOR

Above: The Fleet Air Arm has always carried out its share of rescue duties. In October, 1960, No 719 Squadron, a helicopter training squadron at Eglinton lifted the master of MV *Argo Delos* from his ship, wrecked off Donegal.

Above: HMS *Hermes* commissioned in 1960 as a brand-new carrier. [MOD

Top right: This ship was instrumental in the Kuwait Crisis when its squadron of Whirlwinds (848) put 42 Marine Commandos ashore within a day of the development of the crisis. [MOD

Right: The Supermarine Scimitar replaced the Sea Hawk in 1958, at first with 803 Squadron, subsequently joining 800, 804 and 807 Squadrons. The aircraft's clean lines are shown by this 807 Squadron aircraft, part of the Squadron's display team at Farnborough in 1959. [AUTHOR

Bottom right: Hermes carried 804 Squadron with Scimitars, the familiar tiger's head standing out on the white fins. [B. J. LOWE

Above: A further role was found for the ubiquitous Whirlwind HAS7. With the commissioning of HMS *Bulwark* as a commando carrier (a direct result of lessons from the Suez affair), the Whirlwind was used as a tool for rushing Marine Commandos ashore from the carrier. [AUTHOR

Below: By 1959 the Fleet Air Arm had acquired a British built Early-Warning aircraft to replace the American Skyraider. It was the AEW3 version of the Fairey Gannet, which was used in four-aircraft flights aboard each carrier. One of *Centaur*'s aircraft has just landed and is folding its wings as it is spotted forward. [AUTHOR

Above: An attempt to revive the Swordfish concept, a cheap simple anti-submarine aircraft for baby carriers was evident in the Short Seamew but it was not proceeded with. [VIA B. J. LOWE

Below: More succesful developments took place aboard various frigates. A rudimentary landing platform aft was used by development versions of the Saunders Roe P531 helicopter.

Top left: These were so successful that the helicopter was developed into the Westland Wasp HAS1 capable of carrying depth-charges, torpedoes and frigates provided with platforms to operate them. The Wasps all belonged to 829 Squadron, based at the new helicopter base at Portland, being detached to the ships. HMS *Aurora*'s Wasp over the ship, the landing circle being clearly visible. [MOD

Left: The Wessex also entered the commando role in 1962 and almost immediately HMS *Bulwark*'s 845 Squadron was sent ashore to deal with Indonesia's predatory intentions in Borneo. [MOD

Top: Further helicopter developments brought the Whirlwind a successor in the form of the bigger and more powerful Wessex. This became operational in the anti-submarine role with 815 Squadron in 1961, seen exercising here off Culdrose, the Navy's main helicopter base, prior to embarking in *Ark Royal*. [AUTHOR

Above: The Navy received the ability to deliver a nuclear punch with the entry into service in 1963 of the Blackburn Buccaneer S1. This very advanced aircraft was designed for high-speeds at low-level, a taste practised from the Buccaneer base at Lossiemouth amongst the mountains of Scotland. This 800 Squadron aircraft flies over Sutherland at an unrepresentative 4000ft. [AUTHOR

Above: With blown flaps and dive-brakes wide open a Buccaneer about to thump *Ark Royal*'s deck. The aircraft is over-shooting as the arrester hook is not down. [AUTHOR
Below: In 1964 the Fleet Air Arm assembled itself at Yeovilton for another Royal Review. The helicopters were lined up on one disused runway and fixed-wing aircraft on another beyond the active runway. The weather did not bless the event.

Top: The Fleet Air Arm had already made use of flight refuelling techniques to extend the range of its fighter umbrella by fitting buddy packs to its Sea Vixens. Two of 890 Squadron's Sea Vixen FAW2s are here connected whilst number three is using his under-fuselage dive-brake to position himself in number two's drogue. [C. W. MOGGRIDGE

Above: To extend the range of its Buccaneers No 800 Squadron in 1965 formed a flight of tanker Scimitars. With three underwing tanks and a buddy pack these aircraft topped up the Buccaneer S1s. The frothing emblem on the fin was symbolic of tanking up. [AUTHOR

Top left: During practice over the Moray Firth the Buccaneers did not always hook up first time! [AUTHOR

Middle left: At the same time the Scimitar still fulfilled its strike role with 803 Squadron on *Ark Royal*. The checks on the fin are black and yellow. [AUTHOR

Left: A second carrier was converted to the commando role and she received the first squadron of Wessex HU5s, a twin-engined development of the Wessex giving an added margin of safety in the low-level operations which are the bread-and-butter of a commando squadron. [AUTHOR

Top: Amongst the training aircraft in use in the 'sixties was the Hiller UH12 helicopter used by 705 Squadron at Culdrose and here seen in skittish mood at Culdrose's satellite, Predannack. [AUTHOR

Above: The Sea Venom still served as an observer trainer with 750 Squadron at Lossiemouth. [AUTHOR

Top: Whilst the Hunter in two-seat form as the T8 and single-seat form as the GA11, served as a jet trainer with 738 Squadron at Brawdy.
Above: And as a strike trainer with 764 Squadron Lossiemouth. This GA11, a converted ex-RAF Hunter F4, with rockets on the under-wing racks, leads its number two on to Lossie's runway for a strike on Tain ranges. [AUTHOR

Below: The Buccaneer was re-engined as the S2 and in this form became one of the most potent aircraft in the Western armoury. This aircraft served with 700B Intensive Flying Trails Unit at Lossiemouth in 1965. [AUTHOR

Bottom: 809 Squadron demonstrates the Buccaneer S2's rock-steadiness at low-level at upwards of 500 knots. [AUTHOR

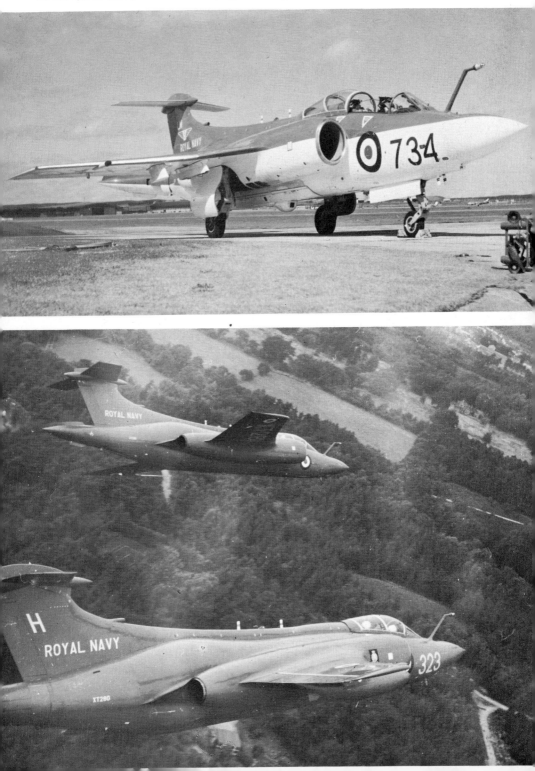

Above: The Fleet Air Arm brought its showmanship to a new high in 1966 when *Hermes* Air Group made the brightest of all the contributions to the SBAC Display at Farnborough. [AUTHOR

Below: In the anti-submarine role the Wessex, in its HAS3 form, was given highly-sophisticated search radar. This 826 Squadron aircraft from HMS *Eagle* is lowering its dipping sonar to the water below. [AUTHOR

Above/Below: One of the small facets of Fleet Air Arm operation has been helicopter support of the British Antarctic bases. This began on HMS *Protector* and is carried on by HMS *Endurance*. Two Whirlwind HAR9s provide a flying force . . . [AUTHOR

. . . with its helicopters fitting in hangars reminiscent of a sardine tin. [AUTHOR

Top left: As the 'sixties progressed various different vessels appeared with helicopter hangars and platforms such as HMS *Engadine* here.

Middle left: The one carrier to receive the Phantom has been the *Ark Royal* after a massive refit to fit her for the task.

Left: As the clouds of extinction gathered around the carrier force the Fleet Air Arm received its most potent aircraft—the McDonnell Douglas F-4K Phantom FG1;

not the 138 ordered but just 28, enough for one squadron plus the training squadron No 767, from which this aircraft comes.
[B. J. LOWE

Top/Above: She has a waist catapult, here about to launch one of 809 Squadron's Buccaneer S2s with massive jet blast deflectors to absorb the reheat of the Phantom . . .
[AUTHOR

. . . there she goes. [AUTHOR

Top: Her anti-submarine force comprises 824 Squadron with Sea King HAS1s providing longer range and more equipment room than the Wessex. [AUTHOR

Middle: Her catapults can punch off a bomb and tank laden Phantom (of 892 Squadron). [MOD

Above: And her decks take the thud of a Phantom's return. [AUTHOR